T0194247

THE CHRISTIAN LIFE

Discovering Your Spiritual Inheritance in Christ

BRENT ADKISSON

WESTBOW
PRESS®
A DIVISION OF THOMAS NELSON
& ZONDERVAN

WestBow Press books may be ordered through booksellers or by contacting:

WestBow Press
A Division of Thomas Nelson & Zondervan
1663 Liberty Drive
Bloomington, IN 47403
www.westbowpress.com
1 (866) 928-1240

ISBN: 978-1-9736-3087-6 (sc)
ISBN: 978-1-9736-3089-0 (hc)
ISBN: 978-1-9736-3088-3 (e)

Library of Congress Control Number: 2018906889

Print information available on the last page.

WestBow Press rev. date: 06/21/2018

CONTENTS

INTRODUCTION

Many view Christianity as another of the world's many religions, just another futile attempt by humanity to find a pathway to God. But true biblical Christianity is no religion at all. The Christian life is a personal relationship with God through His Son, Jesus Christ. It is the fulfillment of God's promises through the patriarchs and prophets of old that offers redemption from sin, liberation from death, and freedom from eternal condemnation.

> John 8:36 | NIV
> Jesus replied, "So if the Son sets you free, you will be free indeed."

The Christian life is a life of freedom. It is a life of freedom from sin, freedom from death, freedom from condemnation and freedom from religion. It was for freedom that Christ has set us free.

The amazing news of the gospel is not simply that we as Christians have received Jesus into our hearts and lives, but that Jesus has received us into His. True freedom can only be found in Christ and as believers we can experience this freedom because we live in Him. All the blessings of God are now available to us because we are in Christ. This is the good news of the gospel of God's grace.

> *John 10:10 | NKJV*
> *Jesus said, "I have come that they may have life, and that they may have it more abundantly."*

The Christian life is a life of abundance. It is a life of abundant faith, a life of abundant love, and a life of abundant hope! In promising believers an abundant life, Jesus is stating, that in Him, we will experience a life that is greater than anything we could ever expect or imagine.

> *John 3:16 | ESV*
> *"For God so loved the world, that He gave His only Son, that whoever believes in Him should not perish but have eternal life."*

The Christian life is an eternal life. This life begins the moment we enter into a covenant relationship with God. It is a life that offers divine protection, provision, power, and spiritual blessings in Christ Jesus.

The Christian life is not about following some impossible list of rules, reciting boring prayers, or repeating some redundant mantras. It is not a life of trying to be good enough to get to heaven, nor is it about doing good deeds to obtain God's approval. Rather it is a life of regeneration and transformation: lost to found, old to new, unrighteous to righteous, darkness to light, death to life, and sinner to saint.

If you have never been a fan of religion, but believe in God, the Christian life is for you! If you have tried the church thing but never experience the presence of God, the Christian life is for you! If you have been a Christian all your life, but have never walked in the power of His Spirit, maybe you're doing it wrong? If you desire a life full of righteousness, peace, and joy, I assure you, the Christian life is for you!

In the chapters that follow, you will be introduced to many spiritual concepts that will strengthen your faith and help you to live the abundant life promised to you by Jesus. Our theme verse will be:

> *Ephesians 5:8 | NKJV*
> *For once you were darkness, but now you are light in the Lord. Walk as children of light.*

How do children of light walk? They walk according to their spiritual identity. If you want to experience success in your Christian walk, you must first understand who you are, what you have, and what you can do as a believer in Christ Jesus. Understanding and applying these biblical truths will transform your life into the image of the one who called you out of darkness and into the light!

CHAPTER 1

Identity Crisis

When I was a child, my mother used to read me a book titled, *Are You My Mother?* by P. D. Eastman. It is a fictional story of a baby bird that hatched while his mother was out getting him some food. As his mother was delayed in her return, the baby bird left his nest and began a journey to find his mother. He found a kitten and asked,

"Are you my mother?"

"No!" the kitten replied; "I am not your mother."

He found a hen and asked,

"Are you my mother?"

"No!" the hen replied; "I am not your mother."

He found a dog and a cow, but they were not his mother. He saw a boat, a plane, and a big machine that went "Snort," but they were not his mother. The search for his mother had been unsuccessful, and now the baby bird was lost and alone. Fortunately, the Snort returned the little birdie to his nest just as his mother returned with breakfast.

The little bird was new to this world and was not sure of who he was or where he belonged. In the search for his mother, he was able to rule out who he wasn't. He was not a kitten or a hen or a dog or a cow or a boat or a plane or a Snort. His search for identity was answered when he found his mother. His mother was a living example of who he was.

We live in a world that struggles with identity. Wandering masses of lost little birdies roaming through the night to find their place in this world. They search for value, purpose, and significance anywhere they can find them.

To experience success in this life, we all must come to understand our purpose from a spiritual and eternal perspective. In the story of Adam, we learn that we were created for relationship with God. Isaiah teaches us that we were created for God's glory. Ecclesiastes reveals that God has placed eternity in our hearts. We were created to live forever, but the human soul was not designed to live outside the presence of God. When we are born into this world, we are born into Adam, not Christ. That is why all of us must be born again. Living outside of a covenant relationship with God creates a huge identity vacuum.

The solution to our identity crisis can only be found in Christ.

Sadly, many people today believe that they have the power to fix this problem on their own. In their search for significance, they attempt to find their identity in this world rather than turning to God.

Some attempt to find their identity in relationships.

The emptiness we experience in our souls is the result of being out of relationship with God. Many do not understand their need for God, but they do perceive that relationship is something they are missing. Relationships are good. Connection, intimacy, family, and community are all good for the soul, but human relationships are not able to fill the space that belongs to God.

Some attempt to find their identity in their heritage.

"I am British!"
"I am Canadian!" (Oh Canada!)
"My father is Irish! That's why I have a short temper!"

Some attempt to find identity in their astrological symbol.

"I am a Gemini!"
"I am a Pisces!"
"I am an Aries! That's why I'm so bossy!"

Some attempt to find their identity in physical appearance.

"I'm a blond!"
"I'm a brunette!"
"I'm a red head! That's why I'm so spicy!"

Some attempt to find their identity in a career.

Many people become workaholics, neglecting their families as they try to find purpose in their career accomplishments or cultural acceptance through their net worth.

Some attempt to find their identity in alternative lifestyles.

It's a strange world we live in today. People identifying as things they are not, trying to be original or unique. Men identifying as women, and women identifying as men. Men identifying as dogs, and women identifying as cats. But in the Creator's eyes, our species and gender are not negotiable traits.

Some attempt to find their identity in a bottle or a pill.

The use of drugs and alcohol may be able to change the way you think, act, and feel, but these changes are only temporary and leave the substance abuser worse in the end. Attempting to find or change your identity through drugs and alcohol is a true recipe for failure.

Some attempt to find their identity in negative lifestyles.

There are some in our world today who are so empty and wrecked from abuse and neglect, that they have resorted to negative lifestyles, such as victimization, physical abuse, sexual abuse, or even spiritual abuse to fill their emptiness. They embrace an abusive lifestyle and endure the pain because it makes them feel wanted.

Finding identity in any of these things may bring temporary satisfaction, but only a covenant relationship with the Creator can truly satisfy this void. Your identity can only be found in Christ. We were created by God - and we were created for God. According to the Bible, our relationship with God begins with spiritual birth.

> *John 3:5-7 | NLT*
> *Jesus replied, "I assure you, no one can enter the Kingdom of God without being born of water and the Spirit. Humans can reproduce only human life, but the Holy Spirit gives birth to spiritual life. So, don't be surprised when I say, 'You must be born-again.'"*

As humans, we are born of the seed of man, but to become a Christian, you must be born-again of the Seed of God.

> *1 Peter 1:23 | NKJV*
> *Having been born-again, not of corruptible seed but incorruptible, through the Word of God which lives and abides forever.*

The Law of the Seed.

In all of God's creation, identity has a direct correlation to a seed. A mustard seed produces a mustard plant. A grape seed produces a grapevine. An apple seed produces an apple tree. And each bears fruit according to its kind. This same concept applies to our spiritual lives. **When we were born-again, we took on the identity of the spiritual Seed from which we were born.** Our spiritual identity comes directly from God, and this new identity is revealed to us throughout New Testament scripture.

One of the most important things to know about our spiritual identity is that we are new! The Bible declares that we are brand-new creations in Christ Jesus. The old is gone, and the new is here! Outwardly, we may resemble our moms or our dads, but our spiritual identity is not the product of the DNA passed down to us from our earthly parents. **In Christ, we are completely new!** We now possess the spiritual DNA of our Creator. We are not who we used to be. We are new creations, new spiritual people, and children of light.

> *Ephesians 5:8 | NKJV*
> *For you were once darkness, but now you are light in the Lord. Walk as children of light.*

As believers, we are light! This is our new spiritual reality. If we could see into the spirit realm who we were prior to salvation, we would only see darkness, but now in Christ, we are light. Before Christ, in Adam, we were unrighteous, but now in Christ, we are righteous. In Adam, we were spiritually dead, but in Christ, we have been given new life, and with this new life, we now possess a new spiritual identity. Let's explore below the surface of the new you.

You are spirit!

Your spirit is the real you. God is also Spirit. To have a relationship with God, you had to experience a spiritual birth. The Bible refers to this new birth as regeneration. This happened when you were born-again. The born-again you is the real you. You have eternal life in Christ because you are a child of God and your spirit will live forever.

> *Romans 8:16 | NKJV*
> *The Spirit Himself bears witness with our spirit that we are the children of god.*

You are a spirit, and you have a soul!

Your soul is made up of your mind, your will, and your emotions. Fortunately, your soul does not determine your identity. That is good news because your soul is fickle and can change at any time. Choosing to base your identity on your soul is a sure recipe for disaster.

Your soul is constantly changing as it reflects on both internal and external information. You can change the way you think. You can change the way you feel. You can change the way you respond to situations. These changes in your soul may affect the way others perceive you, but they do not change your spiritual identity.

You are spirit, you have a soul, and you live in a body!

Our bodies are very temporary. Compared to eternity, our earthly lives are just a bleep, just a vapor. Here today, gone tomorrow. The Bible refers to our bodies as tents, temporary earthly dwellings. Yet we as short-sighted humans seem to focus most of our time and energy on our temporary physical bodies.

You can change a lot about your body. You can modify your physical appearance. You can cut and style your hair. You can adorn your body with nice clothes or fine jewelry. You can get bigger, and you can get smaller. For some reason, getting bigger seems much easier. But changing the characteristics of your physical body will never change your identity. Changing your style, your look, your size, or your shape can never change who you are.

This is because who you are is not the result of some physical attribute. Your identity is spiritual and cannot be changed by some outward presentation. True identity is internal; it is spiritual, and it is determined by a Seed.

Do not allow your flesh to define who you are. Do not allow your culture to define who you are. Do not allow your career to define who you are. Do not allow your family or friends to define who you are. Let God define who you are and allow His Word to be the sole source of your identity.

You are a child of God.

> *Galatians 3:26 | NIV*
> *So, in Christ Jesus you are all children of God through faith.*

And as a child of God you have inherited a new identity. Seeing yourself through the mirror of God's Word is the only identity that matters. Your purpose is directly connected to your identity and this is part of your spiritual inheritance in Christ. Your new identity is solid and secure because it is rooted in His Word, and His Word will never fail. You have been born-again of a spiritual Seed, the Word of God, which lives and abides forever.

CHAPTER 1 REVIEW QUESTIONS

1. Prior to salvation, how did your identity crisis negatively impact your life?

2. What areas do you seek to find identity apart from Christ?

3. Why did Jesus say, "You must be born-again?"

4. What is *The Law of the Seed?*

5. When you look into the mirror of God's Word, how do you answer the question, "Who am I?"

6. Why is it not wise to base your identity on your emotions?

7. Since your spiritual identity influences your behavior, what are you doing to change your perceived identity?

CHAPTER 2

Old vs. New

The contrast between the Old and New Covenants is one of my favorite studies in the entire Bible. The Bible is a compilation of seven different Covenants. The two most recorded are the covenant God made with Israel through Moses, referred to as the Old Covenant, and the covenant God made with born-again believers through Jesus, called the New Covenant.

There are significant differences between the Old Covenant and the New Covenant. These are two independent systems with completely different purposes. The old system brings death, while the new system gives life. The old system was rooted in law, while the new system is rooted in grace. The old was works-based, while the new system is faith-based. Understanding the nature of the covenant through which we are in relationship with God can help us to experience the fullness of our relationship with Him.

Let's begin with the Old Covenant, also referred to as the Law of Moses. This covenant was given to Moses and the children of Israel in the Sinai wilderness seven weeks after their exodus from Egypt. God gave Israel a long list of rules in the form of commandments or laws and then established blessings and curses based on their behavior. When Israel obeyed God and followed His rules, the result was blessings and provision. When they turned their back on God and failed to obey His instructions, the result was curses, destruction, captivity, and death.

The Law of Moses was a merit-based system and blessings were the direct result of obedience to the terms of that covenant.

The Old Covenant was God's idea, and the terms of this covenant were God's divine instructions to the children of Israel.

> *Romans 7:12 | NKJV*
> *The Law is holy, and the commandment holy and just and good.*

The problem with the Law of Moses is that it was powerless to make us holy, just, and good. Yet, the Law of Moses is a significant piece of God's masterful plan of redemption.

> *Hebrews 8:7 | NLT*
> *If the first covenant had been faultless, there would have been no need for a second covenant to replace it.*

It is interesting to read God's take on these two covenants. There is a considerable amount of Old Testament prophecy about the New Covenant, but the most significant portion is found in the book of Jeremiah. Here 600 years before Christ, God reveals His plan to make this New Covenant. The Book of Hebrews says that the New Covenant is better, and in Jeremiah, God explains why!

> *Jeremiah 31:32 | NLT*
> *This covenant will not be like the one I made with their ancestors when I took them by the hand and brought them out of the land of Egypt. They broke that covenant, though I loved them as a husband loves his wife,"*
> *says the Lord.*

God says the New is not like the Old.

The Old Covenant was a conditional covenant where the blessings and promises of God were dependent upon the obedience of the children of Israel. God was obligated to keep his part of that covenant which included punishment in the form of curses upon His chosen people for their disobedience. God had promised abundance, provision, protection, and blessings upon the nation of Israel, but God was unable to deliver on His promises because of their disobedience. They broke the terms of that covenant and never received the promised blessings that God had desired to give to them. The Old Covenant ended on the Cross when Jesus cried out, "IT IS FINISHED!"

The New Covenant is not a conditional covenant like the Old. The New Covenant is a completely different type of covenant called a Testament, which is a will. I'm sure you've heard of a Last Will and Testament! Well, that's the type of covenant God made through Christ. At the last supper Jesus proclaimed that His Blood was to be the Blood of the New Covenant. Hebrews tells us that a testament goes into effect only after the death of the testator. Jesus is the Testator (originator or giver) of the New Covenant and His death on the Cross opened the door to a new and better Covenant. Better because the blessings of a testament are not works-based, they are not Law-based, and they are not conditional. The blessings and promises of a Testament are inheritance-based. Under the terms of the New Covenant, God's blessings are no longer dependent upon our obedience. These blessings are part of our spiritual inheritance. They are a gift from God. We receive them by grace through faith when we trust in Jesus and enter into a New Covenant relationship with God.

The New Covenant is a different type of covenant. It is not a merit-based system. Blessings are not the result of good deeds or works, and in the New Covenant, there are no curses. The only curses you will find in the writings of the New Testament are in the book of Galatians, and those curses are upon anyone who teaches New Covenant believers to follow the rules of the Old Covenant.

Many have asked why Jesus was required to be circumcised, observe the Law of Moses, and keep the Sabbath and Jewish festivals. If Jesus is our example and He obeyed all the terms of the Old Covenant, shouldn't we do the same? It's a great question and the answer is something that every believer should understand.

Jesus did not live under the New Covenant!

There is a page in most Bibles found between Malachi chapter 4 and Matthew chapter 1 that reads, "The New Testament." To better understand the scriptures as they pertain to each covenant, it would be wise to remove this page from your Bible and insert it between John chapter 21 and Acts chapter 1.

Why? Because the people and events recorded in the gospels were all subject to the Old Covenant Law of Moses.

> *Galatians 4:4 | NKJV*
> *But when the fullness of the time had come, God sent forth His Son, born of a woman, born under the Law.*

The gospel period, which records the life and ministry of Jesus, was under the jurisdiction of the Old Covenant. Jesus was born under the authority of the Law. He lived a perfect life under the authority of the Law and died a perfect death under the authority of the Law. In doing so, He fulfilled the righteous requirement of the Law on behalf of Israel, who had failed to keep the terms of the Law and constantly violated God's covenant. It was the death of Jesus on the Cross that enacted the New Covenant and it was delivered to His followers seven weeks later, on the day of Pentecost as described in Acts chapter 2.

The Book of Acts is where we first see the New Covenant in action. As Christians, when we are born-again, we are born into the jurisdiction of this New Covenant. Jesus was born into the Covenant of Law, and He was responsible to observe the terms of the Old Covenant. We are born into the covenant of grace and we are responsible to observe the terms of the New Covenant. Nowhere within the pages of the New Covenant will we find instructions to keep the Law of Moses, the Jewish Sabbath, nor the Jewish Festivals. We are not under that old rule-based system. The Old Covenant demonstrates God's love, mercy and faithfulness, but it does not contain instructions for living the Christian life. It is not wise to look into the Old Covenant for instructions on how to live as a believer. Those instructions were specific to that time, that culture, that people group and that covenant.

Anyone who tries to live the Christian life according to the instructions of the Old Covenant, rule-based system, will be greatly disappointed. Mixing these two systems creates chaos and confusion. Once we receive new spiritual life through the gospel of God's grace, it is not a good idea to submit ourselves to the old system that was the ministration of death and condemnation.

Why does New Covenant scripture refer to the Old Covenant as the ministry of death and condemnation?

Let me explain: Redemption is a two-part system. The old system convicted the world of sin and pronounced a sentence of death and condemnation upon all. This system had to be in place prior to the Messiah coming to earth. How could Jesus pay the price for our sins if that price had not yet been determined? The Old covenant was the legal system which set the price of the ransom that must be paid to redeem humanity from the curse of sin. The old system brought death. The new system gives life.

With that in mind, it's easy to see why the Bible says the New Covenant is better and superior to the old! These are two completely different types of Covenants with different purposes. The Old Covenant was works-based while the New Covenant is inheritance-based. I would compare the difference to having a rental contract on a home versus a homeowner's deed. The Old Covenant is like a rental contract on a home. It comes with lots of rules and restrictions, plus it requires a regular monthly payment. The New Covenant is like a homeowner's deed. The debt has been paid and the old contract has been stamped "PAID IN FULL!"

The Old Covenant was a conditional contract based on laws and works. The New Covenant is a different type of contract called a Testament, as in "Last Will and Testament." Yes, it is a will, rooted in grace, and because it is a testament, it is inheritance-based. All the blessings of the New Covenant, including eternal salvation and the gift of the Holy Spirit, are received upon entrance into this covenant. We cannot earn these blessings, as they are a gift from God.

> *Ephesians 2:8-9 | NKJV*
> *For by grace you have been saved through faith, and that not of yourselves; it is the gift of God, not of works, lest anyone should boast.*

You cannot earn salvation. You cannot earn God's blessings. You cannot earn your spiritual inheritance because it is a gift from God. This is why God chose to make the New Covenant a testament, as it was all a part of His masterful plan of redemption.

How do you receive salvation? How do you receive justification? How do you receive reconciliation? It's all a gift from God and it is available to anyone who chooses to repent of his or her old sinful lifestyle and enter into this New Covenant relationship with God through Jesus Christ.

> *Hebrews 9:14-15 | NLT*
> *For by the power of the eternal Spirit, Christ offered Himself to God as a perfect sacrifice for our sins. That is why He is the One who mediates a New Covenant between God and people, so that all who are called can receive the eternal inheritance God has promised them.*

Here is where religious people get all freaked out! "No more rules?" "That's lawlessness!" Religious folk are addicted to the fleshly gratification that comes from believing that their good behavior has something to do with their righteousness. Jesus called this the righteousness of the Pharisees and told His followers that this type of righteousness could not get them into the kingdom of heaven. Many religious-minded people today do not understand the difference between the covenants. They simply fail to understand the significance of the role of the Holy Spirit in the New Covenant.

One part of our spiritual inheritance is our new identity in Christ. As Christians, we don't live according to a list of rules; we live according to our new identity in Christ. We don't live according to our old sinful nature; we live according to our new spiritual nature. We have been born-again of the Seed of God and we now produce fruit in accordance with our new nature. We don't need a rental contract instructing us not to destroy our house. We inherited the house and we take good care of it because it's ours. We own it.

The absolute best part of our spiritual inheritance is the promise of the Holy Spirit. Jesus sent the Holy Spirit as a Helper and a Comforter. He is always with us. He leads us into all truth. He will never leave us, and He will never forsake us. The old system of rules could only command us to love others. Under God's new and better system, the Holy Spirit shows us who needs love, when they need love, and how we can love them in their current situation. The old system of rules may have been a good moral compass, but the Holy Spirit is far superior. He is not just some mapping tool, but our own personal tour guide in this adventure called the Christian Life. He is always with us and daily leads us in paths of righteousness.

God never offered the Old Covenant to any of the Gentile nations. It was an exclusive covenant offered to the nation of Israel and the descendants of Abraham through his son, Isaac. There are Jews today who still adhere to many of the teachings in the Old Covenant Law. This religious practice is called Judaism. God has a special plan for Israel. Christians have great love and respect for the nation of Israel. I, for one, do not have a problem with Jews who observe their cultural traditions. I do take issue with those who teach that Christians must practice Judaism. Christianity is not Judaism. It is not a revised Judaism. It is not a modified form of Judaism. Christianity is a completely new and different covenant between God and all who choose to have faith in Jesus Christ for salvation. If anyone ever tells you that God expects you to convert to Judaism and observe the terms of the Old Covenant Law of Moses, tell them, "No, thank you!" The New Covenant was God's idea and He says it's better!

If you would like to read more on this subject, please check out *The Book of Covenants.*

CHAPTER 2 REVIEW QUESTIONS

1. What type of covenant is the Old Covenant?

2. How is the New Covenant different from the Old?

3. What event marked the end of the Old Covenant?

4. On what day was the New Covenant given to Christ's followers?

5. How is living according to your spiritual identity better than following a list of rules?

6. Why is the Holy Spirit a better *moral compass* than the Law?

7. In your own words, explain why the New Covenant is better than the old?

CHAPTER 3

Sinner Saved by Grace

In our journey to discover who we are, it will be helpful to rule out who we are not. Believing we are a turkey when God made us an eagle will have a negative effect on our ability to soar. Possessing a wrong belief of who we are will often hinder our ability to live in the fullness of God's plan for our lives.

Often, we hear Christians proclaim, "I'm just a sinner saved by grace!" I've even heard pastors speak this from the pulpit and I cringe just a little bit every time I hear it.

Maybe you've said this yourself. It sounds like a statement of genuine humility, and many who utter this humble saying do so with noble intentions. But what does it mean to be a sinner saved by grace? Isn't that an oxymoron, like "Living Dead," "Jumbo Shrimp," or "Peacekeeper Missiles?"

A Christian who claims to be a sinner is like a butterfly that claims to be a caterpillar. They are completely ignoring the redemptive work of Jesus on the Cross. They are rejecting the process of regeneration. They are denying the fact that they were born-again.

If a person who is a sinner repents of their sin and receives the gift of salvation by grace, are they still a sinner?

The answer is no! According to the scriptures, there is no such thing as a righteous sinner or an unrighteous saint. Spiritually and biblically this is not possible.

And another important biblical truth that we need to consider before referring to ourselves as a "sinner saved by grace" - sinners don't go to Heaven!

> *1 Corinthians 6:9-11 | NIV*
> *Or do you not know that wrongdoers will not inherit the kingdom of God? Do not be deceived: Neither the sexually immoral nor idolaters nor adulterers nor men who have sex with men nor thieves nor the greedy nor drunkards nor slanderers nor swindlers will inherit the kingdom of God. And that is what some of you were. But you were washed, you were justified in the name of the Lord Jesus Christ and by the Spirit of our God.*

Did you catch that last part? "And that is what some of you were." This statement refers to something you were in the past tense; once you were sinners. Then it goes on to say, "But you were washed, you were justified." This is also in the past tense. What does it mean to be justified? The biblical definition is *to be declared righteous* by God. But if you are a simple person like me, it's okay to defined it as, *just as if I had never sinned!* You were a sinner prior to your new birth and you were justified at the time of regeneration. Now, thanks to the Blood of Jesus, you are not who you used to be!

Biblically speaking, the word sinner is synonymous with being unrighteous. Justification is the legal transformation from sinner to saint. And the word saint is equated with the word righteous. In Paul's letter to the Ephesians he did not address these New Covenant believers as *the sinners in Ephesus*. No, he writes to *the saints in Ephesus!*" And in his letter to the Romans, Paul explains just how we all became sinners and how we can be made righteous.

> Romans 5:19 | NKJV
> For as by one man's disobedience many were made sinners, so also by one Man's obedience many will be made righteous.

It was Adam's disobedience that made you a sinner. This was part of your earthly inheritance from the seed of Adam at your natural birth. It is the obedience of Jesus that makes you righteous. Righteousness is a part of your spiritual inheritance from the Seed of Christ when you were born-again.

And here is where the theological arguments begin!

"Well, if I sin, doesn't that make me a sinner?"

My sarcastic response; "If I go golfing, does that make me a golfer?"

The answer to both questions is, "No!"

The argument and the answer can both be found in the book of 1 John.

> 1 John 1:10 | NKJV
> If we say that we have not sinned, we make Him a liar, and His word is not in us.

This verse is referring to our past; "If we say we have not sinned." We have all sinned. Every one of us was born of the seed of Adam and inherited a sin nature. It should not come as a surprise to anyone that sinners sin! And we are all aware that some of us were better at it than others. The question here is, what is our relationship to sin after regeneration? Do saints sin?

Let's look at what John says about this issue:

> *1 John 3:9 | NKJV*
> *Whoever has been born of God does not sin, for His seed remains in him;*
> *and he cannot sin, because he has been born of God.*

And just to make sure we didn't miss this important truth, John makes the same claim again just two chapters later.

> *1 John 5:18 | NKJV*
> *We know that whoever is born of God does not sin.*

If you've never seen this important truth before, you may be a little confused right now.

Whoever is born of God DOES NOT SIN?

Wow! How can this be? Who are these super Christians John is referring to? They must have been some type of early Church Christian Ninjas or something!

But you have to realize that this is the same John who penned these words of Jesus:

> *John 3:6-7 | NKJV*
> *"That which is born of the flesh is flesh, and that which is born of the Spirit is spirit. Do not marvel that I said to you, 'You must be born-again.' "*

These two different births are responsible for two separate parts of who we are. We are both flesh and spirit.

The *whoever* in 1 John 3:9 and 1 John 5:18 is not referring to the natural, fleshly person. The *whoever* is referring to the born-again believer, the new creation, and the spiritual child of light. John is telling us that our spirit does not sin. We inherited the nature of God through His spiritual Seed. Our new spiritual nature is a reflection of His divine nature.

If we do a quick word study in our concordance on this word translated as *whoever*, we will find that this same Greek word can also be translated as *whatever*. *Whoever* is the correct translation because this verse is referring to a person, but when we discover that this word can also be translated as *whatever*, we are then able to understand the concept of what part of us these verses are referring to. When we read this verse as *Whatever is born of God does not sin*, it brings to light what John is referring to. The part of us that was born of God, the God-begotten part of us that was created in righteousness and holiness, this is the part of us that does not sin.

The apostle Paul confirms this same idea when he says,

Romans 7:20 | NKJV
Now if I do what I will not to do, it is no longer I who do it, but sin that dwells in me.

This verse further explains the disconnect between the flesh and the new spiritual nature. He is identifying with his spiritual nature when he claims that he is not the one sinning, but it is the sin that dwells in his fleshly nature. It is important to understand that when we struggle with the flesh, we are struggling against the old way of thinking. Our old way of thinking needs to be washed by the water of God's Word. This is where renewing the mind becomes critical in the sanctification process.

Do we sometimes struggle with the temptation to sin? Yes! We still live in a fallen world dominated by sin, and there is an adversary who does not want us to succeed. The struggle is real. We must continue to war against those carnal desires that are contrary to right living. But we do not allow the temptation or the struggle to define who we are. Before Christ, we were ruled by sin, but in Christ we are free! Sin no longer has dominion over us. God's grace empowers us to walk in righteousness and we are free from sin's control.

> *Romans 6:14 | ESV*
> *For sin will have no dominion over you, since you are not under the Law but under grace.*

The only power that sin has over you today is the power that you give it.

Through the fleshly nature inherited from Adam, we all experience failures and shortcomings. Focusing too much on those areas of failure only seems to empower them. One of the devil's schemes is to get our mind off of Jesus by enticing us to dwell on our past failures. Nowhere in the scriptures are we instructed to dwell on our past. We are to fix our eyes upon Jesus. He is the source of all we are and all we hope to be. We will experience victory over our failures and fleshly desires as we walk in the Spirit and embrace our new spiritual identity.

> *2 Corinthians 5:16 | NKJV*
> *Therefore, from now on, we regard no one according to the flesh.*

This includes the way we see ourselves.

In Adam, we sinned because it was a part of our fleshly identity and carnal nature, but in Christ we are new. In Adam we were unrighteous, but we have been made the righteousness of God in Christ Jesus. In Adam, we were unholy, but in Christ we have been created anew in true righteousness and holiness. We have inherited a new identity and a new nature. We no longer regard ourselves according to the flesh. We no longer identify with the old fleshly nature. We were born-again into Christ. We now abide in Him, and in Him there is no sin!

> *Ephesians 5:8 | NKJV*
> *For you were once darkness, but now you are light in the Lord. Walk as children of light.*

You were a sinner. That was your old fleshly identity. You have been saved by God's grace. That is the miraculous process of redemption purchased for you by Jesus on the Cross.

1 Corinthians 6:11 | NKJV
But you were washed, but you were sanctified, but you were justified in the name of the Lord Jesus and by the Spirit of our God.

And now thanks to your New Covenant inheritance in Christ Jesus, you are a saint!

CHAPTER 3 REVIEW QUESTIONS

1. When a sinner gets saved by God's grace, are they still a sinner?

2. Whose disobedience made us all sinners?

3. Whose obedience makes us saints?

4. When we accept Christ, what part of us is born again?

5. What does it mean to be justified by God's grace?

6. Why does sin no longer have dominion over us as believers? *Romans 6:14.*

7. What does it mean that we *regard no one according to the flesh? 2 Corinthians 5:16.* How then should we perceive fellow believers?

CHAPTER 4

Conformed vs. Transformed

> Romans 12:2 | NKJV
> Do not be conformed to this world, but be transformed by the renewing of your mind.

As New Covenant believers, we are instructed to not be conformed or pressed into the image that the world would like us to be. Society sets a narrative as to how we should live in this world. Unfortunately, most of the prominent voices in our world today are not submitted to God or His Word. The world has its own version of right and wrong and often those standards fall short or even contradict God's instructions for right living. God's standards of living are not subject to the whims of cultural opinion. As Christians, we are not to live according to the expectations of this God-less society.

> *1 Peter 1:13-16 | ESV*
> *Therefore, preparing your minds for action, and being sober-minded, set your hope fully on the grace that will be brought to you at the revelation of Jesus Christ. As obedient children, do not be conformed to the passions of your former ignorance, but as He who called you is holy, you also be holy in all your conduct, since it is written, "You shall be holy, for I am holy."*

I love that! "Preparing your minds for action!" You will never be a successful Christian on accident. You must live with purpose, focused on the prize. The apostle Paul compares the Christian life to training for the Olympics. I've never had the opportunity to speak with a gold medal winner about their training regimen, but I'm pretty sure that they didn't restrict their training to Sundays. No, they trained every day and they had to give up on some of the pleasures of life to remain committed to their goal of winning.

> *1 Corinthians 9:24 | NKJV*
> *Do you not know that in a race all the runners run, but only one gets the prize? Run in such a way as to get the prize.*

As followers of Jesus we are to conduct our lives in such a manner that our actions will produce success! This will only come about as we prepare our minds for action and exchange our old way of thinking for God's right ways of thinking. In Christ Jesus, we have abandoned the fleshly desires of this world. We now live the set apart life as children of God, where we operate with purpose, seeking first the kingdom of God and His righteousness.

> *Colossians 3:2-3 | NLT*
> *Think about the things of heaven, not the things of earth. For you died to this life, and your real life is hidden with Christ in God.*

Anyone who is born-again and filled with the Spirit of Christ will have a conviction and a passion for living a pure and holy life. Yet many believers struggle with sin, addiction, and strongholds that often leads to frustration and hopelessness. The problem may not be a lack of desire to do good, rather a lack of understanding of how to turn that desire into action. How do we move from a desire to be holy to walking in holiness? How do we get from bondage to freedom? How do we get from failure to success? How do we get from sinner to saint?

I was sitting in a home Bible study years ago and the group leader was harping on the participants that they just needed to love God more. After his fifth appeal to the group to just love God more, I interrupted and simply asked, "How?" Initially my question was met with silence, then he responded, "Keep His Commandments!"

That my friends is religion! Christianity is a relationship. Jesus said, "If you love Me, keep my instructions!" He did not say, if you keep my instructions, you will love me. Obedience does not produce love. Love produces obedience. We obey God because we trust Him, and we trust Him because we understand how much He loves and cares for us. Essentially, we love Him because He first loved us! And because we love and trust Him, we choose to live a set-apart life.

It's obvious that in our pursuit of God, we do not want to be conformed to the ways of the world system. But equally important, we don't want to make the mistake of being conformed to a religious system of works.

Religion tells us it's all about obeying the rules. "Don't drink, don't cuss, don't chew, and don't hang around with those who do!" Religion may be able to modify some of your behavior, but it does not have the power to change who you are.

Religion does not produce godliness. The life that we seek to live as believers can only come from our covenant relationship with God. It is the transforming power of the Holy Spirit that enables us to walk in Holiness, righteousness and freedom.

Our actions do not determine our identity, but our identity should influence our actions!

Trying to follow a list of rules without renewing your mind will only result in frustration and failure. Even the best Old Covenant system of rules, the Law of Moses, was unable to produce holiness, godliness, or a new life.

The only way to live a holy life is to do it God's way. Success will only be discovered as we allow the truth of the Word to change the way we think and believe about ourselves.

> *Romans 12:2 | NLT*
> *Don't copy the behavior and customs of this world, but let God transform you into a new person by changing the way you think.*

Have you ever wondered why your pastor is always telling you to read your Bible?

It is because he understands that transformation is the result of renewing our minds. When we renew our minds to the truth of the Word of God, we allow the Holy Spirit to transform our lives by bringing our heart and mind into alignment with our new God given identity.

> *Ephesians 4:23-24 | NLT*
> *Let the Spirit renew your thoughts and attitudes. Put on your new nature, created to be like God—truly righteous and holy.*

When we do it the right way, when we do it God's way, when we do it the way New Testament scripture instructs us to, we will experience a new lifestyle of righteousness and holiness.

So how exactly does this *right way* work?

We shall begin with this concept of holiness, but this pertains to everything the Bible declares about you through your spiritual inheritance.

The Bible says that we were created in holiness. This is not something that our carnal minds want to accept, so we must plant that truth in our hearts like a seed. That seed will need good ground to grow in, which is soil made up of faith in God, confidence in His Word, and assurance of His promises. This is our part of the equation and is a conscious choice that we must make. We must prepare the soil of our hearts to receive, then sow the good seed of God's Word into that good ground. This seed will take root and begin to grow. We don't have to make it grow. It is a seed and that's what seeds do; they grow. As the seed grows and matures, we will experience a new awareness and understanding that holiness is now a part of who we are. This process is called the renewing of the mind. It is the process of changing how we think about ourselves. It is the mental transition from our old identity as inherited from Adam to our new identity as inherited from Christ. This is not brain washing. This is a spiritual process designed by God and empowered by His Spirit to give the believer right thinking, which will in turn produce right living. As the Word of holiness grows in our hearts and our minds are renewed, that word will begin to produce the fruit of holiness in our daily walk. The greater the soil (faith and confidence in God's Word), the greater the harvest.

Let's look at our verse again and add in verse 1 to add a little to the context:

> *Romans 12:1-2 | NKJV*
> *I beseech you therefore, brethren, by the mercies of God, that you present your bodies as a living sacrifice, holy acceptable to God, which is your reasonable service. And do not be conformed to this world but be transformed by the renewing of your mind.*

This transformation process begins with us. God does not operate in us against our will. We must choose to surrender to God and place our lives upon the altar. We must present ourselves to God as a living sacrifice. Another translation says that this is our spiritual act of worship!

As we present ourselves before God, He takes what we give Him, and He transforms us into who He wants us to be. The word *transformed* is a very interesting word in the original text. Strong's G3339 is the Greek word *Metamorphoō*. This is the same word that was used to describe what happened to Jesus in Matthew 17 when the Glory of God came upon Him and he was *transfigured* while on top of the mountain with Peter, James and John. This word is used two other times in the Bible in reference to Christians and both times it is translated as *transformed*. It is a verb and is only used in the passive tense.

Why is that significant?

This transformation process is not of our own doing. This is not something that God expects for us to do, nor is it something we have the ability to do. It is the work of the Spirit of Christ in us, transforming us into His image. Yes, our spiritual transformation is God's responsibility. He is the only one who has the power to change a life from sinner to saint. Our responsibility is to believe His promise, trust His Word, and submit ourselves to His Spirit.

> *2 Corinthians 3:18 | NIV*
> *And we all, who with unveiled faces contemplate the Lord's glory, are being transformed (Metamorphoō) into His image with ever-increasing glory, which comes from the Lord, who is the Spirit.*

This supernatural transformation process is of the Lord's doing. The Holy Spirit is the transformer of our lives. We are being changed into His image and this process comes with a bonus of "ever-increasing glory" from the Lord. The process of transformation and increase of Glory takes place as our minds are renewed to the truth of God's word pertaining to our new spiritual identity.

Do you want to live a Holy life? Get your mind renewed to the truth that you are created in true righteousness and holiness. In the process, your walk will be transformed by the Spirit of the Lord who not only said, "You shall be holy, for I am holy," but has declared you to be holy, renewed your mind to your new identity as being Holy, then transformed your life to a place where you now walk in holiness!

Do not be conformed to the world! Do not be conformed to religion! Allow the Word of God to renew your mind and allow the Spirit of God to transform your life with ever-increasing glory!

Romans 12:2 | NKJV
Do not be conformed to this world, but be transformed by the renewing of your mind, that you may prove what is that good and acceptable and perfect will of God.

CHAPTER 4 REVIEW QUESTIONS

1. Why is rule keeping not able to change your identity?

2. What does it look like to be conformed to the world?

3. What does it mean to, *run in such a way to receive the prize*?

4. What determines your identity?

5. Many Christians have been conformed to a religious system. Why does this not produce eternal change?

6. Explain the significant difference between brain washing and mind renewal?

7. Why is it important that the verb *transformed* is passive?

CHAPTER 5

Who Are You?

You will often hear people make the claim that we are all God's children. That sounds good and it's a nice thought, but it's completely unfounded according to the Word of God. The truth is that we were all born of the seed of Adam and we were all born into sin.

Are unbelievers the children of God?

> John 1:12-13 | NKJV
> As many as received Him, to them He gave the right to become children of God, to those who believe in His name: who were born, not of blood, nor of the will of the flesh, nor of the will of man, but of God.

No, unbelievers are not the children of God. They are the children of the flesh, the children of Adam, or even worse!

> 1 John 3:10 | NLT
> So now we can tell who are children of God and who are children of the devil.

This passage suggests that it is one or the other. Either you are a child of God, or you are a child of the devil.

There is a very interesting discourse found in the Gospels between Jesus and some of the Pharisees. These Pharisees were esteemed throughout Israel for their commitment and dedication to following the Old Covenant Law. You couldn't find a more religious, rule-keeping group of folks than these Pharisees. **But look what Jesus says about who they are:**

> *John 8:44a | NIV*
> *"You are of your father the devil."*

Yes! Jesus said that. And these Pharisees were Israelites, the direct descendants of Abraham who were strict observers of the Torah. How could these children of Abraham not be the children of God?

> *Galatians 4:4-7 | NLT*
> *But when the right time came, God sent His Son, born of a woman, subject to the Law. God sent Him to buy freedom for us who were slaves to the Law, so that He could adopt us as His very own children. And because we are His children, God has sent the Spirit of His Son into our hearts, prompting us to call out, "Abba, Father." Now you are no longer a slave but God's own child. And since you are His child, God has made you His heir.*

Those under the Law of Moses were not considered to be the children of God. This is because redemption from the Law was a prerequisite to becoming a child of God. Jesus came to buy freedom for those who were under the Law so that they could become God's children. If you do a quick search through your bible for "the children of God," you will find that this title is used a dozen times in the New Testament, but it is not found anywhere in the Old Testament. Being a child of God is a New Testament concept. Scripture often refers to the Jewish people as the children of Israel or the Children of Abraham, but not the children of God. In order to be a child of God, we must be born-again.

> *Romans 9:8 | NLT*
> *This means that Abraham's physical descendants are not necessarily children of God. Only the children of promise are considered to be Abraham's children.*

This is because you are not a child of God until you are born-again of the Seed of God.

> *1 John 5:1 | ESV*
> *Everyone who believes that Jesus is the Christ has been born of God!*

New Covenant believers are the only ones the Bible refers to as the children of God.

> *Galatians 3:26 | NIV*
> *So in Christ Jesus you are all children of God through faith.*

And this is the position from which we receive our new identity in Christ.

> *Romans 8:16-17 | NKJV*
> *The Spirit Himself bears witness with our spirit that we are children of God, and if children, then heirs—heirs of God and joint heirs with Christ.*

As children of God, we are heirs of God and joint heirs with Christ! Heirs of what, you might ask?

> *1 John 4:17 | NKJV*
> *As He is, so are we in this world.*

We have inherited a new identity that makes us like Jesus! Yes, our new identity reveals that in Christ, we have become like Jesus. As Christians, we are like Christ not because of our works, but because we have received a new spiritual DNA. Who else would we be like after being born of the Seed of God? The law of the seed is that a seed always produces fruit after its kind. Our new spiritual nature and identity are the direct result of the Seed who gave us new spiritual life.

There was a time in my Christian journey when I did not understand the concept of spiritual identity. I remember an exciting yet frustrating season in my life when I knew God was trying to teach me something, but it just wasn't clicking in my head. I read and studied my Bible every day and although I was aware of many of the elements of my identity in Christ, there was no revelation. The light had not turned on. Then, after months of feeling like I was on the edge of spiritual breakthrough, I came across this verse.

> *Ephesians 5:8 | NKJV*
> *For you were once darkness, but now you are light in the Lord. Walk as children of light.*

The light of revelation turned on in my mind and my walk with God has never been the same.

In my mind, I had always interpreted this verse as "once you were *like* darkness, now you are *like* light." I thought this was an analogy or a metaphor. But this verse does not say we are *like* light. It says that we are light. This is a reality of our spiritual identity in Christ.

One reason new believers have a difficult time living a bible-based life is because they have no idea who they are. James says that the Bible is like a mirror to show us who we are. Many look into the Word of God, see who they are, then walk away and forget what they look like.

When we look into God's Word we see the reflection of who we really are. Our spiritual identity is a part of our spiritual inheritance as New Covenant believers.

To answer the question, "Who are you?" all you need to do is take a look in the spiritual mirror of God's Word!

I am born of God — 1 John 5:18

I am a child of God — John 1:12

I am a new creation — 2 Corinthians 5:16

I am an heir of God — Galatians 4:7

I am a joint-heir with Christ — Romans 8:17

I am holy — Colossians 1:22

I am blameless — Ephesians 1:4

I am righteous — 2 Corinthians 5:21

I am a saint — Ephesians 1:1

I am God's temple — 1 Corinthians 3.16

I am a citizen of heaven — Philippians 3.20

I am God's workmanship — Ephesians 2:10

I am Christ's friend — John 15:15

I am a member of Christ's body — 1 Corinthians 12:27

I am a member of a royal priesthood — 1 Peter 2:9

I am a minister of reconciliation — 2 Corinthians 5:18

I am sealed by the Holy Spirit — 2 Corinthians 1:22

I am complete in Christ — Colossians 2:10

I am a Christian because spiritually I am like Christ — 1 John 4:17

This is the image that we, as believers in Christ, see when we behold ourselves in the mirror of His Word. And none of this is of our own doing. This is our inherited identity. It is a gift from God.

Our spiritual identity is not just for our own personal consumption. God has given us this identity through spiritual inheritance for a purpose. He desires for us to live like Jesus, love like Jesus, and be His hands and feet as we share the hope of the Gospel to a lost and dying world.

> John 14:12 | NKJV
> "Most assuredly, I say to you, he who believes in Me, the works that I do he will do also; and greater works than these he will do, because I go to My Father".

Jesus prophesied that we would do equal and greater works than He did. He desires that for all of us who believe in Him. Knowing who we are and understanding our spiritual identity will empower us for success as we serve the Lord through the ministry to which He has called us.

The book of James teaches us that our tongue is like a rudder on a ship that sets the course of our life. Don't be afraid to confess the truth of your spiritual identity. If you are struggling with living in the abundance of your inheritance, confession could help you get your victory.

> *Proverbs 18:21 | NKJV*
> *Death and life are in the power of the tongue.*

When we confess our God-given spiritual inheritance in Christ, we are speaking His promises, and those promises produce life.

Who are you?

You are a child of the King. You were born into royalty. You were created by God and for God to do great works in the kingdom of God.

> *1 John 3:1-2 | NKJV*
> *Behold what manner of love the Father has bestowed on us, that we should be called children of God! Therefore, the world does not know us, because it did not know Him. Beloved, now we are children of God.*

God loves you!

CHAPTER 5 REVIEW QUESTIONS

1. Why are the physical descendants of Abraham not the children of God?

2. Who are the true children of God?

3. *1 John 4:17* says, *As He is, so are we in this world.* What does that mean to you?

4. *Ephesians 5:8* says that as believers we are light. What part of our makeup is this referring to?

5. How does your reflection as seen in the mirror of God's Word differ from the image you hold of yourself?

6. The Bible is clear that we are royalty in Christ. How should this affect the way we daily think and live?

7. What is the result when we base our identity on our emotions? How can we solve this problem?

CHAPTER 6

Pride vs. Humility

In my early years of ministry, I had a friend who was a great youth pastor at a nearby church. My youth services were on Wednesday evenings and his youth services were on Thursdays. I would rarely miss an opportunity to be a part of his meetings.

His teaching style was much different than mine. I taught biblical doctrines with practical applications while he was more philosophical and evangelistic. My personal conviction was to always have something new to teach each week. He on the other hand liked to preach using stories that he would repeat and refine over time. Both of us taught a lot on the subject of sin and living a pure life, as that seemed to be a struggle for many during their high school and college years.

One message that I always looked forward to was his philosophical approach to living a life free of sin. After a string of questions that revealed the sinful behaviors of his audience, he would put forth this challenge;

Can you go 1 second without sinning?
Can you go 10 seconds without sinning?

Can you go 1 minute without sinning?
Can you go 10 minutes without sinning?
Can you go 1 day without sinning?
Can you go 10 days without sinning?

And then he would cap it off with a verse like:

Hebrews 12:4 | NKJV
You have not yet resisted to bloodshed, striving against sin.

We were all very young and still learning the basic biblical concepts of the Christian faith. We were unaware of our inheritance in Christ. We had not been introduced to the truth of our spiritual identity. We did not know that in order to change our actions, our minds must first be renewed by the Word of God. We did not understand that the transformation process was the divine work of the Holy Spirit in our lives. We thought that everything was our responsibility and because of our ignorance, we were trying to do this on our own, the old way, by following a bunch of rules.

Fortunately, we were born again and had received the promise of God's Holy Spirit.

John 16:13 | NLT
When the Spirit of truth comes, He will guide you into all truth.

We were zealous for the things of God, although we did lack wisdom. My pastor once told me that God could do more through a person who is abundant in zeal and lacking in wisdom, than a person full of wisdom who lacked zeal. God blessed our enthusiasm to serve Him and enabled us to reach thousands of youth with the message of the Gospel. We were daily in His Word and our hearts were open to Him. Those were great times in the presence of God and as I look back, I think God was as excited about our spiritual journey as we were.

I am grateful for the power of the Holy Spirit working in my heart and leading me into His truth. It was during that season of my life where God began to teach me about identity. My spiritual walk was unleashed as I discovered this life changing truth. I didn't have to live according to some long list of do's and don'ts, trying to be holy. God had already made me holy when He put a new heart and a new spirit in me. All I had to do was be me, the new me, the real me, the spiritual me!

Once I learned the truth, it didn't take me long to accept, embrace, and begin to live according to my identity in Christ. This new revelation was life changing and I began to teach this message of God's goodness everywhere I went.

It wasn't long before I ran into those who didn't agree with this message. It was the *woe is me, I'm so unworthy, just a sinner saved by grace* crowd. They believed that it was prideful and arrogant to believe these things about yourself. Their justification was the story that Jesus told of the Pharisee and the tax collector.

Here is this story:

> *Luke 18:9-14 | NLT*
> *"Two men went to the Temple to pray. One was a Pharisee, and the other was a despised tax collector. The Pharisee stood by himself and prayed this prayer: 'I thank You, God, that I am not a sinner like everyone else. For I don't cheat, I don't sin, and I don't commit adultery. I'm certainly not like that tax collector! I fast twice a week, and I give You a tenth of my income.'*
> *"But the tax collector stood at a distance and dared not even lift his eyes to heaven as he prayed. Instead, he beat his chest in sorrow, saying, 'O God, be merciful to me, for I am a sinner.' I tell you, this sinner, not the Pharisee, returned home justified before God. For those who exalt themselves will be humbled, and those who humble themselves will be exalted."*

Let's look at the Pharisee in this story. He has based his identity in his own deeds. He is good at following all the rules. His righteousness is a righteousness of works. He appears to do all the right things. But Jesus says that this Pharisee is exalting himself and living in pride.

Self-exaltation is equated with self-righteousness and this is not an acceptable way to approach God.

When we identify with who we are in Christ, we are not bragging on ourselves, we are bragging on Jesus. Christianity is not self-righteousness as none of this is of our own doing. Everything we are is because of Jesus. We are holy, righteous, forgiven, justified, purified, and born-again solely because of the perfect work of Jesus Christ. When we believe, receive, and walk in our new identity, we are exalting Christ.

Now let's take a look at the tax collector. He said, "O God, be merciful to me, for I am a sinner."

The central message of Jesus was, "Repent for the kingdom of Heaven is at hand." John says,

> *1 John 1:9-10 | NIV*
> *If we confess our sins, he is faithful and just and will forgive us our sins and purify us from all unrighteousness. If we claim we have not sinned, we make him out to be a liar and his word is not in us.*

This tax collector was a sinner. He cried out to God for mercy. And what does Jesus say was the result of his petition before God? "I tell you, this sinner, not the Pharisee, returned home justified before God."

What a great story of the grace and mercy of God! Jesus came for the sinner, and this sinner was justified because he placed his trust in God and cried out for mercy.

Let's explore once again what it means to be justified? Justification is being declared righteous by the Judge. At salvation, God makes a declaration over your life, and when God speaks, it becomes reality. Justification is a key element of our spiritual inheritance. The tax collector wasn't declared righteous by God because he was good at following the rules.

God declared him righteous because of his faith! And Jesus said that God exalted him because of his humility.

After we have repented of our sin, received salvation, regeneration, and justification, is it still humility to call ourselves unworthy, unrighteous, or sinners? No, that is false humility because this is no longer an accurate depiction of who we are. Jesus said,

> Matthew 5:20 | NKJV
> "For I say to you, that unless your righteousness exceeds the righteousness of the scribes and Pharisees, you will by no means enter the kingdom of heaven."

The Pharisee was self-righteous because of his own works. He put his confidence in himself and Jesus said this was self-exaltation or pride. The tax collector cried out for mercy and was declared righteous by faith. He placed his confidence in God and Jesus defined that as humility. God is honored when we acknowledge the miraculous work of Jesus.

True humility is believing what the Bible says about us!

Bragging to God about how great we are to earn his approval is pride. Bragging to God about how wretched, miserable, and worthless we are to earn His approval is false humility. Confessing that He is God and He is our source of everything that is good is true humility. It's futile to approach God in false humility. Our value has already been determined. Like a work of art, our eternal worth was established 2000 years ago.

God established your eternal value when He paid the price for your redemption.

What is your value? What are you worth to God? You are worth the price that God chose to pay for you (His only Son). The Bible says that you are His masterpiece and to Him, you are priceless! Stop arguing with God. He's not going to change His mind.

As New Covenant believers, we place our faith, hope, and confidence in Jesus. When we receive our spiritual inheritance and accept our identity in Christ, we have entered into a position of humility as we acknowledge that none of this is because of us. This is all God's doing. Our inheritance is a gift from Him!

As your mind becomes renewed to your identity in Christ, you will experience an increased level of boldness and confidence in your Christian walk. Some may mistake this boldness as arrogance but as we just discussed, this confidence is not born out of pride, rather revelation of the Truth of God's Word. Jesus is our perfect example.

> *Philippians 2:5-8a | NKJV*
> *Let this mind be in you which was also in Christ Jesus, who, being in the form of God, did not consider it robbery to be equal with God, but made Himself of no reputation, taking the form of a bondservant, and coming in the likeness of men. And being found in appearance as a man, He humbled Himself and became obedient to the point of death.*

Religious people cannot think, act, or love like Jesus did. They are too insecure in themselves and too afraid of what people might think of them. Jesus knew who He was; He was secure in His relationship with the Father and He was confident in His identity. He did not need to prove anything to anyone. He was not insecure about His purpose here on earth. Because of this, He was able to humble Himself, take on the role of a servant, and live a life of obedience. The Bible says that we are to have this same mind or attitude in our Christian lives.

Once you get the revelation that you are a child of God and you have the approval of your Heavenly Father, you will not need to seek the approval of others. It is difficult to humble yourself and love selflessly like Jesus loved when you are insecure with who you are. When we live for the approval of others it opens the door to manipulative and controlling relationships which are a form of bondage. But Jesus came to set us free. As we obey the instructions of Philippians 2:5 to think like Jesus, we will experience victory over our insecurities. This Christ-like attitude will position us to humble ourselves and serve others in the full capacity to which God has called us to serve.

As we allow the mind of Christ to influence our walk, we will be able to serve others from a pure heart full of God's love, grace, mercy, and truth. As we humble ourselves before God, He will raise us up, just as He did with Jesus.

CHAPTER 6 REVIEW QUESTIONS

1. Where did the Pharisee find his identity?

2. Why does rule keeping produce pride?

3. What approach did the tax collector take before God to cause him to return home justified?

4. What type of righteousness exceeds the righteousness of the scribes and Pharisees?

5. What is true humility? To whom is it expressed?

6. What is false humility? To whom is it expressed?

7. Why is it difficult for insecure people to serve others? How do we overcome these insecurities?

CHAPTER 7

Everything You Need

Discovering our new spiritual identity as a born-again child of God is essential to living a Spirit-filled life. We have discussed what the Bible says about **who we are** in Christ and discovered that our identity is a part of our spiritual inheritance. Knowing our spiritual identity is a great start, but it is just the first step in learning how to walk in the Spirit. Let's explore **what we have** as believers that enables us to successfully live the Christian life.

When we believed in Jesus and repented of our sins, we were born-again into the kingdom of God. Our New Covenant relationship with God is rich in spiritual blessings. So, what does the Bible say about what God has already given us? As we search the pages of New Testament scripture, we will discover that through inheritance, God has thoroughly equipped us with everything we need to live a victorious Christian life.

> *2 Peter 1:3 | NIV*
> *His divine power has given us everything we need for a godly life.*

Please note the verb tense in this Bible promise. We are not sitting here on Earth waiting for God to equip us for our spiritual journey. We do not need to spend hours in prayer begging Him to give us the power to live this life. His divine power has already given us everything we need for life and godliness. We already have it!

When we began this journey with Jesus, most of us were not real sure where our Christian walk was leading us. And we didn't know what tools we might need to help us reach our destination. The good news is that God knew everything we would need for this journey and has provided all of this to us in Christ.

> *Ephesians 1:11 | ESV*
> *In him we have obtained an inheritance!*

> *Colossians 1:12 | NLT*
> *He has enabled you to share in the inheritance that belongs to His people, who live in the light.*

Again, look at the verb tense in these verses. Religion has taught us that we will have everything we need once we get to Heaven, but the Bible says the blessings of Heaven have been given to us here in this life, so we can experience a little bit of Heaven here on Earth. ***Thy kingdom come, Thy will be done, on Earth as it is in Heaven,*** was not just a cute prayer that Jesus taught His disciples. This kingdom belongs to us. As Christians, the kingdom of God has come, and it lives in us! We are already royalty in that kingdom because we are the children of the King. We are not waiting for the end of this life to receive our inheritance. We already have it!

Many believers are missing out on God's best because they have believed a lie that we must suffer through this life on Earth, so we can go to Heaven and experience God's blessings. But is that what Jesus promised us? Think about it! Life does not begin at death. Life begins at birth, and eternal life begins at spiritual birth. God doesn't want you to wait until you get to Heaven to experience your new life in Christ. He wants you to live and enjoy that abundant life right now.

> *John 10:10 | NKJV*
> *"I have come that they may have life, and that they may have it more abundantly."*

If we want to experience this abundant Christian life as promised by Jesus, we will need to understand exactly what tools He has given us for this journey.

In Chapter five we explored *who we are* in Christ. Now it's time to look at *what we have* as a result of our spiritual inheritance.

What does the Bible say that we have been given in Christ?

We have eternal life through Jesus - 1 John 5:11

We have redemption through His blood - Colossians 1:14

We have been justified by faith - Romans 5:1

We have been delivered from the powers of darkness - Colossians 1:13

The love of God has been poured out in our hearts - Romans 5:5

We have direct access to God through the Holy Spirit - Ephesians 2:18

We have a promise of an abundant life - John 10:10

We have boldness - Ephesians 3:12

We have been sealed with the Holy Spirit - Ephesians 4:30

We have been sanctified – 1 Corinthians 6:11

God has given each of us the measure of faith - Romans 12:3

We have a sound mind - 2 Timothy 1:7

We have power - Acts 1:8

We have forgiveness of our sin - Colossians 1:14

We have a personal advocate with the Father - 1 John 2:1

We have peace with God - Romans 5:1

We have grace in Him – 2 Timothy 1:9

We have a spirit of love - 2 Timothy 1:7

We have an anointing from the Holy One – 1 John 2:20

We have all of the promises of God – 2 Corinthians 1:20

We have been blessed with every spiritual blessing - Ephesians 1:3

This is all a part of our spiritual inheritance in Christ and is God's promise to us through His covenant, the New Testament, that is a will. These promises are bequeathed to us at the point of regeneration. All of these blessings, including the promise of the indwelling Holy Spirit, are gifts to strengthen, encourage, and empower us to live an abundant and godly life.

> *Hebrews 9:15 | NIV*
> *For this reason, Christ is the mediator of a New Covenant, that those who are called may receive the promised eternal inheritance.*

The Bible refers to our spiritual inheritance as blessings. And those blessings have already been given to us by God through the New Covenant. This fact should raise a couple of questions: Where is this inheritance? And how do we obtain our blessings?

> *Ephesians 1:3 | NKJV*
> *Blessed be the God and Father of our Lord Jesus Christ, who has blessed us with every spiritual blessing in the heavenly places in Christ.*

So, it's like the Pot o' Gold at the end of the rainbow?

No! This is not some mystical treasure that is unobtainable. It's your inheritance and the Bible declares that it is already yours in Christ.

> *Ephesians 2:3-6 | ESV*
> *But God, being rich in mercy, because of the great love with which He loved us, even when we were dead in our trespasses, made us alive together with Christ — by grace you have been saved — and raised us up with Him and seated us with Him in the heavenly places in Christ Jesus.*

We are not working to obtain the blessings of God. As New Covenant believers, we have been blessed with "Every Spiritual Blessing" and all of those blessings are found in Christ.

As believers, *where* does the Bible say that we are **spiritually**?

We are *seated in the heavenly places in Christ Jesus.* This is a spiritual reality found in New Testament scripture. We may not completely understand it, but this is true of us regardless. Like much of our spiritual identity, we must trust God's Word even when we cannot see it. The Holy Spirit will bring understanding as we choose to walk in faith.

There are some religious types out there who do not agree with this message of spiritual inheritance. They insist that, like Israel, we must earn our blessings through a system of works. God knew this would be the case and the Bible explains why these people do not understand this wonderful message of God's grace.

Let's take a moment and look at the spiritual realities prior to, and after the Cross.

> 1 Corinthians 2:9 | NKJV
> But as it is written:
> "Eye has not seen, nor ear heard, nor have entered into the heart of man the things which God has prepared for those who love Him."

This was the spiritual reality for Israel before the Cross. But after the Cross, everything changed. Look at the new spiritual reality found in the next verse.

> 1 Corinthians 2:10 | NKJV
> But God has revealed them to us through His Spirit.

What has been revealed to us through His Spirit?

The things which God has prepared for those who love Him.

> 1 Corinthians 2:12-14 | NLT
> And we have received God's Spirit, so we can know the wonderful things God has freely given us. When we tell you these things, we do not use words that come from human wisdom. Instead, we speak words given to us by the Spirit, using the Spirit's words to explain spiritual truths. But people who aren't spiritual can't receive these truths.

Our spiritual inheritance is not some man-made, feel-good doctrine. The New Covenant was God's idea and *the wonderful things God has freely given us* are revealed to us both through scripture and by revelation as the Spirit of God teaches us about the heart of God. And this is the same Spirit who has given us **everything we need for life and godliness.**

> *2 Peter 1:3 | ESV*
> *His divine power has granted to us all things that pertain to life and godliness, through the knowledge of him who called us to his own glory and excellence.*

What do we have in Christ? We have everything we need to live the Christian life.

We serve a great and awesome God!

CHAPTER 7 REVIEW QUESTIONS

1. What was your motivation for coming to Jesus?

2. Has your Christian journey been exactly what you expected?

3. When does eternal life in Christ begin?

4. When do the promises of our spiritual inheritance begin?

5. Where are our spiritual blessings located? *Ephesians 1:3.* Positionally, where are we seated as believers? *Ephesians 2:6.*

6. In *1 Corinthians 2:9-10,* what is revealed to us by God's Spirit?

7. What are you doing to incorporate God's blessings into your daily spiritual journey?

CHAPTER 8

Legal vs. Vital

Jesus said that all who believe in Him would experience rivers of life. Yet many today feel like they are living in a mud puddle of religion. How can the Bible promise us so much, yet we exhibit so little? Where is this river? Where is this fountain? Where is the abundant life that Jesus came to give us?

Have you ever wondered why one person becomes a Christian and changes the world, while another becomes a Christian and can't even change their emotional diapers? They both received the same inheritance, the same ability, the same power and the same Spirit of God, yet one excels while the other wallows. Why is this?

Many Christians today do not reflect the image portrayed of them in God's Word. They live more like the old sinner they were prior to regeneration than the new saint that they are in Christ. Why do so many Christians live defeated, empty, and boring lives contrary to their God-given inheritance? Maybe it's because they don't know who they are. Or maybe it's because they have never discovered their inheritance in Christ.

Let's step away from the spiritual for a moment and look at inheritance in the natural realm.

Is it possible that some rich distant relative could include us in his will and leave us a fabulous estate plus a bank account stuffed full of cash as an inheritance? Ok, it's highly unlikely, but it is possible. Now, what if we never opened the letter from the attorney's office notifying us of our inheritance. We live our entire lives broke, bankrupt, homeless, and ignorant of what legally belongs to us. Are we still an heir? Yes, legally we could be a multi-millionaire. Yet we could die on the streets from malnutrition or starvation.

That would be a very sad story, but sadly enough, this is the spiritual reality for many Christians today. Believers in Jesus are heirs of an abundance of promises and blessings from God, but they never open the letter from God to find out what legally belongs to them.

When it comes to walking in the Spirit, understanding this next concept could mean the difference between living an abundant life in faith and the power of the Holy Spirit or living a mundane and uneventful Christian life.

It is important to understand the fact that redemption has two parts, the legal and the vital.

The legal part of our redemption is that which is true of every born-again believer in Christ Jesus. Who are we? What do we have? And what can we do since we are in Christ? This is everything promised to us in the Word of God and everything made available to us when the Holy Spirit showed up and took residence in our spirit. The legal part is everything that is now true of us after entering into this New Testament relationship with God.

The vital part of redemption is what we, by faith, appropriate into our daily Christian walk. It's great to inherit spiritual wealth, but we must believe, receive, and incorporate this into our daily living if we want to experience God's best for us. This transfer from legal to vital is essential to walking in the revelation of our spiritual inheritance.

This verse is the perfect example of legal vs. vital.

> Ephesians 5:8 | NKJV
> For you were once darkness, but now you are light in the Lord. Walk as children of light.

"For once you were darkness!"

Our past identity was darkness. Spiritually, we were darkness.

"But now you are light in the Lord!"

Our inherited identity is light. Spiritually, we are light. This is not of our own doing. It is simply a part of our inheritance in Christ.

"Walk as children of Light!"

By faith in Christ and the power of His Spirit, we now appropriate our new spiritual identity into our Christian walk.

How do children of light walk?

If you read on, Paul says, as we discern what is pleasing to the Lord, we take no part in the unfruitful works of darkness, but instead expose them. Children of light reject the old way of living, embrace their new identity, and walk in the light.

This verse now becomes a model for how we move from our legal reality into the vital and walk out our new identity.

The Bible is not instructing us to do something that we cannot do. It is not commanding us to be something that we are not. On the contrary, the Bible has clearly defined who we are and is instructing us to live according to our new identity. In Christ, we are light, and we are expected to walk according to our new spiritual reality.

With that in mind, let's explore this concept of legal vs. vital using our model.

Once you were. Now you are. Therefore walk.

Let's apply this to our salvation.

Once you were: There was a point in everyone's lives when they were not saved. This was the period of time prior to regeneration.

Now you are: In Christ, we are saved. It is a gift from God and we don't have to work for it. This is because salvation is part of our spiritual inheritance as a believer. This is the legal part of redemption.

> *Ephesians 2:8 | NKJV*
> *For by grace you have been saved through faith, and that not of yourselves; it is the gift of God.*

Therefore walk:

> *Philippians 2:12 | NKJV*
> *Work out your own salvation with fear and trembling.*

Here is the vital part of salvation. This verse does not say we must *work for* our salvation. It does say we must *work it out*. Salvation is in us, but we need to make it a vital part of our lives. We need to work it out, walk it out, and live it out.

Remember the song, "If you're happy and you know it, clap your hands?" Well, I added a verse to that song a few years back that says, "If you're happy and you know it, tell your face!" Have you ever known a person who was saved, but their face wasn't? This person needs to work out their salvation. God didn't light our lamp so we could hide it from the world. He wants us to let our light and our salvation shine for all to see.

In order for us to appropriate our identity from the legal to the vital, we will need to reprogram our soul to accept the truth of our spiritual inheritance. This will allow us to faithfully walk according to our spiritual reality.

Once you were. Now you are. Therefore walk.

Let's apply our model to holiness.

The Bible, in one verse, tells us that we are holy, and in another verse, instructs us to be holy. Now if we fail to understand the legal vs. vital concept, this may seem confusing. But when we look into that mirror of God's Word and by faith believe and receive the truth of our identity, we can then appropriate our new identity into our spiritual walk.

> *Ephesians 1:4 | ESV*
> *He chose us in him before the foundation of the world, that we should be holy and blameless before him in love.*

In Christ, you are holy. It is part of your spiritual inheritance. This is a legal aspect of redemption.

> *Ephesians 4:24 | NKJV*
> *Put on the new man which was created according to God, in true righteousness and holiness.*

The new you was created in true righteousness and holiness. But you must put that on. This is the vital aspect of your redemption.

> *1 Peter 1:15 | NKJV*
> *As He who called you is holy, you also be holy in all your conduct.*

This is where we walk out who we are. We can walk in holiness because we were created by God in true righteousness and holiness.

In order to get our vital life to line up with our legal spiritual identity, we must change the way we think. Again, we see the importance of renewing our minds. And renewing the mind only comes about as we spend time with the Holy Spirit, studying the truths of God's Word.

> *Romans 12:2 | NLT*
> *Don't copy the behavior and customs of this world, but let God transform you into a new person by changing the way you think.*

As we renew our mind, we are reprogramming our soul to operate according to our new spiritual identity. As our thoughts and attitudes are changed to God's perspective on things, our lifestyle will be transformed into the image reflected of us in the Word of God. Again, this is why renewing of the mind is such a critical component of the sanctification process.

When the Bible instructs us to put on something, it is usually referring to taking something from the legal and transferring it to the vital, taking the spiritual and bringing it into the natural, and embracing the unseen so that it might be seen.

> *Ephesians 4:24 | ESV*
> *Put on the new self, created after the likeness of God in true righteousness and holiness.*

And here is the same instruction, just stated a little differently.

> *Colossians 3:10 | NLT*
> *Put on your new nature, and be renewed as you learn to know your Creator and become like Him.*

It is expected that children will imitate their parents. This idea is no different with our spiritual Father.

> *Ephesians 5:1 | NKJV*
> *Therefore, be imitators of God as dear children.*

As we live out our inherited spiritual identity we will naturally produce good fruit that demonstrates whose child we really are. God is honored when we walk in our new identity and imitate Him. So, let us renew our minds to the Word of God and allow the Holy Spirit to transform our lives into the image of Christ.

CHAPTER 8 REVIEW QUESTIONS

1. How would you explain the legal part of redemption?

2. What is the vital part of redemption?

3. According to *Ephesians 5:10-11,* how do children of light walk?

4. What does it mean to *work out your salvation?*

5. Is it possible to *be holy as I am holy* without walking in your spiritual inheritance? What can you do to walk in holiness?

6. What does it mean to *put on* your new identity? *Ephesians 4:24, Colossians 3:10.*

7. What characteristics of God would you like to imitate more in your life?

CHAPTER 9

I Can Do All Things

We have learned what the Bible says about **who we are**. We have learned what the Bible says about **what we have** in Christ. Now it's time to explore what the Bible says about **what we can do** as born-again believers who are filled with the power of the Holy Spirit.

Is there anything that God has asked us to do as believers that He has not empowered us for or enabled us to do?

Philippians 4:13 | NKJV
I can do all things through Christ who strengthens me.

Everything that God asks of us, He has already equipped us to do through our spiritual inheritance. Everything that His New Covenant instructs us to do, He has already empowered us to do through His Spirit.

So, *what can we do* when we walk in our spiritual inheritance? We can do everything that God asks us to do!

> *James 4:7 | NIV*
> *Submit yourselves, then, to God. Resist the devil, and he will flee from you.*

We can do this! The devil is not happy when we make the decision to embrace our inheritance and walk in our new identity. He will attack us with who we used to be and may even use others to remind us of our past. We must be fully submitted to God and to the truth in His Word. As we resist his lies, he will flee to find an easier target.

> *John 15:4 | ESV*
> *Abide in Me, and I in you. As the branch cannot bear fruit by itself, unless it abides in the vine, neither can you, unless you abide in Me.*

We can do this! We must always acknowledge that everything we have as believers is a gift from God. He is our source. Outside of our relationship with God, we cannot produce good fruit. But as we live in Christ, we will produce the fruit of His Spirit.

> *Galatians 5:16 | NKJV*
> *I say then: Walk in the Spirit, and you shall not fulfill the lust of the flesh.*

We can do this! When we walk in our spiritual inheritance, being led by the Spirit of Christ, we can overcome the desires of the flesh.

So often we battle against our flesh in order to walk in the spirit. But the Bible teaches the exact opposite! We don't drive out the darkness to reveal the light. We shine the light to expose those things hidden in darkness. When we learn to walk in the spirit, the result will be a life that gives us victory over our fleshly desires.

> *Matthew 11:28-30 | NLT*
> *Then Jesus said, "Come to Me, all of you who are weary and carry heavy burdens, and I will give you rest. Take My yoke upon you. Let Me teach you, because I am humble and gentle at heart, and you will find rest for your souls. For My yoke is easy to bear, and the burden I give you is light."*

We can do this! One of the greatest things we can ever do as Christians is to stop trying to figure everything out on our own and just go to Jesus. To take His yoke upon us means that we join His team. Life is no longer about me, me, me. We are working together for a greater purpose, the kingdom of God.

> *Ephesians 4:32 | NIV*
> *Be kind and compassionate to one another, forgiving each other, just as in Christ God forgave you.*

We can do this! Yes, it can be difficult at times, but God has given us a new heart of kindness and compassion. When we receive and experience God's forgiveness, we will know how to forgive others.

> *Romans 12:9-10 | NKJV*
> *Let love be without hypocrisy. Abhor what is evil. Cling to what is good. Be kindly affectionate to one another with brotherly love, in honor giving preference to one another.*

We can do this! This sounds a lot like living as a child of light. We love with genuine love. We expose the evil and we embrace what is good. Then we love others from a pure heart as Jesus loved.

> *Matthew 5:16 | ESV*
> *In the same way, let your light shine before others, so that they may see your good works and give glory to your Father who is in heaven.*

We can do this! God is light. We are born-again of the Seed of God and now the Bible says that we are light. Letting our light shine is simply living out who God has made us to be as His children and walking out the blessings of our inheritance.

Galatians 5:1 | NIV
It was for freedom that Christ has set us free. Stand firm, then and do not let yourselves be burdened again by the yoke of slavery.

We can do this! Here Paul is instructing us to live in the freedom that we have been given in Christ. Don't let anyone convince you to return to that old system of rule keeping which he said was a *yoke of slavery.* Jesus said that when the Son sets us free, we are free indeed. We honor the sacrifice of Jesus when we live in His freedom!

Philippians 2:14-15 | NLT
Do everything without complaining and arguing, so that no one can criticize you. Live clean, innocent lives as children of God, shining like bright lights in a world full of crooked and perverse people.

We can do this! As God's children, we have been blessed with every spiritual blessing. If God is our source, then we have nothing to complain or argue about. Our needs are being met by God's Spirit. I love the second part of this scripture!

Live clean, innocent lives as children of God, shining like bright lights.

Living a clean life is a true recipe for success. We should not be trying to figure out what we can get away with or how close to the edge we can get before falling off the cliff. Life is so much better when we submit to God's ways and simply walk in the Spirit.

> *Hebrews 12:14 | NKJV*
> *Pursue peace with all people, and holiness, without which no one will see the Lord.*

We can do this! Yes, some people are difficult. It is going to take the mind of Christ working in us. Many times, we are not living in peace with others because we are not walking in holiness. We must humble ourselves and walk in our new identity.

> *John 13:34 | NIV*
> *"A new command I give you: Love one another. As I have loved you, so you must love one another.*

We can do this! This is not love others as you love yourself. This is loving others the way Jesus loves. Esteeming others, honoring others, giving preference to one another in love.

> *Ephesians 4:29 | ESV*
> *Let no corrupting talk come out of your mouths, but only such as is good for building up, as fits the occasion, that it may give grace to those who hear.*

We can do this! Maturity as a believer is marked by how well we control our tongue. James 3:4-5 says it is like a rudder that determines the course of our lives. Proverbs 18:21 says that life and death are in the power of the tongue. It is our responsibility to speak life over negative situations we encounter.

> *Romans 13:14 | NLT*
> *Clothe yourself with the presence of the Lord Jesus Christ. And don't let yourself think about ways to indulge your evil desires.*

We can do this! There is no better life than living in the presence of Jesus. When we clothe ourselves in His presence we walk differently, we talk differently, and we experience true peace and contentment.

> *1 Peter 5:7 | NIV*
> *Cast all your anxiety on him because he cares for you.*

We can do this! Some have experienced great pain and abuse that has left them damaged and broken. The journey to wholeness can be turbulent, but God says we can do all things through Christ who gives us strength. When we cast our anxiety on Him, He carries the heavy burden and gives us peace sufficient to make it through any situation. God loves His children! He heals the broken hearted and binds up their wounds.

> *2 Corinthians 5:20 | NKJV*
> *Now then, we are ambassadors for Christ, as though God were pleading through us: we implore you on Christ's behalf, be reconciled to God.*

We can do this! As Christians, the Bible says we are citizens of Heaven. We have an assignment here on Earth to represent God and His kingdom. As ambassadors for Christ, we share with others the good news of God's love, grace, mercy and forgiveness.

> *Ephesians 6:10-11 | ESV*
> *Finally, be strong in the Lord and in the strength of his might. Put on the whole armor of God, that you may be able to stand against the schemes of the devil.*

We can do this! We can dress ourselves for this spiritual battle called life. We put on the belt of truth and the breastplate of righteousness. We put on our shoes as preparation to go and share the gospel of peace. We take up our shield of faith and our helmet of salvation. And of course, we take our sword of the Spirit, which is the Word of God. What did we just do? We just dressed ourselves in our inheritance! We are now ready to share the good news with all the world.

> Mark 16:15 | NLT
> And then He told them, "Go into all the world and preach the Good News to everyone."

We can do this! The gospel should not be the best kept secret of our generation. The world needs to hear the good news about Jesus. We don't have to cross an ocean to share the gospel of Jesus. There are plenty of people here in our little worlds who need to hear this message of hope. And it really is good news! There is a new life waiting for anyone who will come to Jesus. As others see us walk in the Spirit and in the abundance of our spiritual inheritance, they will see the life of Christ in us.

There are many more scriptures we could look at, but in each situation, we have the same promise. If God has instructed us to do something, He will also empower us to accomplish it! What can we do in Christ?

> Philippians 4:13 | ESV
> I can do all things through Him who strengthens me.

CHAPTER 9 REVIEW QUESTIONS

1. What are we capable of when we walk in our spiritual inheritance?

2. Why do we need to be yoked to Jesus?

3. What does "clean living" mean to you? What are you doing to experience this in your life?

4. How is the *new commandment* in *John 13:34* different from the old commandment of *love your neighbor as yourself?*

5. What does Jesus do for us when we cast our anxieties on Him? Give a personal example.

6. When we *put on the whole armor of God,* what are we dressing ourselves in?

7. What does the Bible say that we can do as believers?

CHAPTER 10

Faith vs. Works

What is the relationship between faith and works in the life of a New Covenant believer? Is there anything we can do to earn God's favor, forgiveness, or eternal life? Are good works a prerequisite for justification or is salvation purely a product of faith?

These questions arise because over half of the Bible takes place under the covenantal jurisdiction of the Old Covenant Law of Moses. In this Old system of laws and commandments, there were established prerequisites for the children of Israel. Physical circumcision and obedience to the Law of Moses were precursors for righteousness.

Deuteronomy 6:25 | NIV
"And if we are careful to obey all this law before the Lord our God, as he has commanded us, that will be our righteousness."

But those days of righteousness through the works of the Law are ancient history.

Paul, who was born a Jew and lived subject to the Law, declared,

Philippians 3:9 | NLT
I no longer count on my own righteousness through obeying the Law; rather, I become righteous through faith in Christ. For God's way of making us right with Himself depends on faith.

This is because the promises and terms of the New Covenant are completely different than the old. The New Covenant was God's idea, and in Jeremiah 31:32, He says that the new is not like the old.

The doctrine of righteousness by works vs. righteousness by faith is one significant difference between these two covenants. The New Testament is very clear that Christians do not live according to the instructions of that old system.

Romans 6:14 | NLT
You no longer live under the requirements of the Law. Instead, you live under the freedom of God's grace.

The gospel of God's grace has opened a new way for us to be saved. Because of God's great mercy and kindness, we all have access to salvation apart from the works of the Law.

Titus 3:4-5 | ESV
But when the goodness and loving kindness of God our Savior appeared, He saved us, not because of works done by us in righteousness, but according to His own mercy, by the washing of regeneration and renewal of the Holy Spirit.

Salvation is the result of entering into a covenant relationship with God through the Blood of Jesus. God offers salvation to us by grace and all who believe in Christ receive this gift through faith.

> *Ephesians 2:8-9 | NKJV*
> *For by grace you have been saved through faith, and that not of yourselves; it is the gift of God, not of works, lest anyone should boast.*

What is grace? Grace is the unmerited, undeserved, or unearned favor of God. The very nature of grace is contrary to the Old system of works through the Law. So clearly works has nothing to do with a believer's salvation, as there is nothing we can do to earn or deserve God's favor. Look at the next verse.

> *Ephesians 2:10 | NKJV*
> *For we are His workmanship, created in Christ Jesus for good works, which God prepared beforehand that we should walk in them.*

We were created for good works. But those works come after regeneration, not before. Under the old system of Law, right standing with God was a result of obedience to the Law. Under the new system of grace, good works are the result of our righteousness in Christ.

Some have suggested that Paul and James do not agree on the doctrine of faith vs. works. But maybe the confusion is as simple as the use of the word works. Paul uses the word in reference to the old system of Law while James seems to be referring to simple obedience.

> *James 2:14 | ESV*
> *What good is it, my brothers, if someone says he has faith but does not have works? Can that faith save him?*

Both Paul and James were Jews who had lived under that old system of Law. Both men were a part of what we refer to today as Judaism. Under Judaism, converts were required to be circumcised, offer sacrifices to become ceremonially clean, observe the Jewish Sabbath, and participate in the annual feasts in order to be accepted into that system. So, when writing about the terms of the New Covenant, we find both of these

New Testament leaders referring back to a time prior to the Law to find a biblical example of what it means to be justified by faith.

Here is Paul's reference to Abraham:

> *Galatians 3:6-7 | NIV*
> *So also Abraham "believed God, and it was credited to him as righteousness." Understand, then, that those who have faith are children of Abraham.*

And here is James' reference to Abraham:

> *James 2:22-23 | NLT*
> *You see, his faith and his actions worked together. His actions made his faith complete. And so, it happened just as the Scriptures say: "Abraham believed God, and God counted him as righteous because of his faith." He was even called the friend of God.*

Both men agree that Abraham was counted as righteous because of his faith. James emphasizes that Abraham's faith was not a passive faith but an active faith that produced obedience to God. James says this is the type of faith we need as believers. Our lives should be a demonstration of our faith.

> *James 2:19-20 | NKJV*
> *You believe that there is one God. You do well. Even the demons believe—and tremble! But do you want to know, O foolish man, that faith without works is dead?*

James challenged believers to not just talk the talk, but to walk the walk. Simply confessing that you have faith does not make you a believer. It's not enough to just say that you are a Christian. You need to walk it out. Authentic faith manifests itself in obedience to Christ.

There are religious leaders today who teach that (post-salvation) works are completely out of the equation when it come to the Christian life. Many believe that once they say the prayer to accept Jesus, their obligation to the covenant is over and its's just a matter of time until they get to go to heaven. Think about it! That's like standing at the alter and saying, "I do!" to your spouse, then walking away thinking there is nothing else required of you in the marriage relationship. Now if you have never been married, that may sound reasonable, but for anyone who has been married for more than a week, you know that's just a ridiculous idea. Your good works cannot earn your salvation, but your faith and devotion to Christ should be evident through your life.

Jesus said there would be evidence from all who believed in Him.

> *John 14:12 | NIV*
> *"Very truly I tell you, whoever believes in Me will do the works I have been doing, and they will do even greater things than these."*

Let's refer back to our theme verse.

> *Ephesians 5:8 | NKJV*
> *For you were once darkness, but now you are light in the Lord. Walk as children of light.*

A life of faith is a life of action. When we walk according to our identity in Christ, we demonstrate to the world that we are children of light. This is the right kind of faith and produces in us good fruit and good works.

Once we understand that James' use of the word *works* is not in reference to the Jewish Law, then we will see the continuity of doctrine of salvation by grace through faith.

Jesus said,

Mark 16:16a | ESV
"Whoever believes and is baptized will be saved."

Peter said,

Acts 2:38 | NKJV
"Repent, and let every one of you be baptized in the name of Jesus Christ for the remission of sins; and you shall receive the gift of the Holy Spirit."

Paul said,

Romans 10:9-10 | NKJV
If you confess with your mouth the Lord Jesus and believe in your heart that God has raised Him from the dead, you will be saved. For with the heart one believes unto righteousness, and with the mouth confession is made unto salvation.

Paul and Silas said,

Acts 16:31 | NKJV
"Believe on the Lord Jesus Christ, and you will be saved, you and your household."

James said,

James 2:18 | ESV
"Show me your faith apart from your works, and I will show you my faith by my works."

No one is suggesting any connection between salvation and the works of the Law. Salvation in the New Covenant is part of our spiritual inheritance. It is a gift from God. There is nothing any of us can do to earn salvation.

James says that there are two types of faith. One type of faith believes in God, yet this faith does not produce change in a person's life. James says this faith is of no benefit because even the devil believes in God.

There is another type of faith that activates the power of God in our lives. This is the faith in the gospel of Jesus Christ. This is the faith that understands it is the works of Jesus that makes a believer righteous.

> *Romans 1:16 | NKJV*
> *For I am not ashamed of the gospel of Christ, for it is the power of God to salvation for everyone who believes, for the Jew first and also for the Greek.*

This is the type of faith that we want! This is an active faith that produces results. It's the faith in Jesus Christ as our Savior and Lord. This is the type of faith that reaches out and takes hold of the free gift of salvation. This is the type of faith that is pleasing to God.

CHAPTER 10 REVIEW QUESTIONS

1. Are good works a prerequisite for salvation in the New Covenant?

2. What is the relationship between faith and works in the life of a believer?

3. Can a person be saved by grace and the works of the Law at the same time?

4. Was Abraham made righteous because of his faith, or because of his works?

5. Are believers in Jesus made righteous because of our faith or our works?

6. Whose works make us righteous? What is the relationship between the works of Jesus and our spiritual inheritance in Christ?

7. What type of faith do you have? How can you increase that faith?

CHAPTER 11

Walking in The Spirit

For God so loved the world that He gave the gift of His only begotten Son. For God so loved His children that He gave us the Gift of His Holy Spirit. His Spirit is at the center of everything we have and everything we do as Christians.

The key to walking in the Spirit is being in relationship with the Holy Spirit!

> John 16:7 | ESV
> "Nevertheless, I tell you the truth: it is to your advantage that I go away, for if I do not go away, the Helper will not come to you. But if I go, I will send Him to you."

It must have been an incredible experience to live in the days of Jesus. I often think about the Disciples and how their lives were so radically changed because of their relationship with Jesus. I'm certain that none of them wanted the earthly ministry of Christ to come to an end. But Jesus knew what was best for His disciples and for all of us who follow Him. He said it would be better for Him to go away because then the Helper, the Holy Spirit, would come.

The ministry of Jesus was limited by His earthly body. He could only be in one place at a time, and they did not have the technology 2,000 years ago to broadcast His messages around the world.

The Holy Spirit is the Spirit of Christ. The Holy Spirit is omnipresent. This means He is not confined to one place. The advantage that Jesus referred to was the ability for Christ to be with each and every believer as they were sent into all the world to share the great gospel of God's grace.

As Christians, does God's Spirit really live in us? Yes, He does! But when Jesus spoke these words, this idea of God's Spirit living in the hearts of His new creations was a totally new concept.

Prior to the Cross, the Spirit of God lived in the Temple in Jerusalem. The architectural design of the temple was given by God. There were three main parts of the temple. The outer court, the holy place, and the most holy place also referred to as the holy of holies. The Spirit of God lived in the heart of the temple in the most holy place.

The same hour that Jesus died on the Cross, the curtain of the temple was torn in two and the Spirit of God moved out of that Old Covenant Temple. Fifty days later, on the day of Pentecost, God's Spirit was poured out on the disciples and other followers of Jesus.

Peter, in the power of the Spirit, stood up and preached Jesus to the crowds in Jerusalem.

> *Acts 2:38 | NIV*
> *"Repent and be baptized, every one of you, in the name of Jesus Christ for the forgiveness of your sins. And you will receive the gift of the Holy Spirit."*

It was here that God revealed His New Covenant temple. Yes, born-again believers in Jesus are now the earthly dwelling place for God's Spirit. This new temple is made up of three parts, the spirit, soul, and body. The Spirit of God lives in the heart of this temple, the spirit of the believer, which is the new *most holy place* created by God in true righteousness and holiness.

Paul refers to this phenomenon as the great mystery.

> Colossians 1:26-27 | NKJV
> The mystery which has been hidden from ages and from generations, but now has been revealed to His saints. To them God willed to make known what are the riches of the glory of this mystery among the Gentiles: which is Christ in you, the hope of glory.

The great mystery was kept secret for centuries, only to be revealed to New Covenant believers. The mystery is that we are the temple of the Holy Spirit and Christ lives in us!

We can know the heart of God because it is His Spirit who lives in us.

> 1 Corinthians 2:11-12 | NLT
> No one can know a person's thoughts except that person's own spirit, and no one can know God's thoughts except God's own Spirit. And we have received God's Spirit, so we can know the wonderful things God has freely given us.

This is yet another reason why the New Covenant is better. When we repented of our sins and believed in Christ, God gave us a new spirit. Then He sent His Spirit to live in our Spirit. The result being that God now has access to the thoughts and desires of our hearts. And in turn, we now have access to the thoughts and desires of God's heart. This is the ultimate divine relationship that God has made available to every born-again believer.

This is why Christianity is not a religion. It is a covenant relationship with God.

In John 14:16 when Jesus said that He would send a *Helper,* referring to the Holy Spirit, He used an interesting word.

It is Strong's G3875 - *paraklētos*

This word can be translated as Helper, Advocate, Comforter, and Counselor. When used in conjunction with the Greek word for *another,* it is understood to mean *another just like the first!* Jesus said He was sending us another Helper who was just like Him. The Holy Spirit is to serve the same role in our lives as Jesus did in the lives of His disciples.

What does God's Spirit do for us when He comes?

The Holy Spirit guides us in all truth.

> John 16:13-14 | ESV
> "When the Spirit of truth comes, He will guide you into all the truth, for He will not speak on His own authority, but whatever He hears He will speak, and He will declare to you the things that are to come. He will glorify me, for He will take what is Mine and declare it to you."

The Holy Spirit gives freedom.

> 2 Corinthians 3:17 | NIV
> Now the Lord is Spirit, and where the Spirit of the Lord is, there is freedom.

Where is the Spirit of Christ? He is in us and the Bible promises that where His Spirit dwells, there is freedom. Galatians tells us that it was for freedom that Christ has set us free, no longer to be subject to the yoke of slavery. In Christ, we are free from sin, death, and condemnation.

The Holy Spirit is the guarantee of our inheritance.

> *Ephesians 1:13-14 | NKJV*
> *In Him you also trusted, after you heard the word of truth the gospel of your salvation; in whom also, having believed, you were sealed with the Holy Spirit of Promise, who is the guarantee of our inheritance.*

We received our spiritual inheritance when we were born-again into the kingdom of God. God sent His Spirit to seal us for the day of final redemption and to teach us about our inheritance in Christ.

The Holy Spirit prays and intercedes for us.

> *Romans 8:26-27 | NLT*
> *And the Holy Spirit helps us in our weakness. For example, we don't know what God wants us to pray for. But the Holy Spirit prays for us with groanings that cannot be expressed in words. And the Father who knows all hearts knows what the Spirit is saying, for the Spirit pleads for us believers in harmony with God's own will.*

The Holy Spirit gives us power to share the good news of Christ.

> *Acts 1:8 | NIV*
> *"But you will receive power when the Holy Spirit comes on you; and you will be my witnesses in Jerusalem, and in all Judea and Samaria, and to the ends of the earth."*

The Holy Spirit is the anointing who teaches us all things.

> *1 John 2:27 | ESV*
> *But the anointing that you received from him abides in you, and you have no need that anyone should teach you. But as his anointing teaches you about everything, and is true, and is no lie—just as it has taught you, abide in him.*

The Holy Spirit pours out the love of God in our hearts.

Romans 5:5 | NKJV
Now hope does not disappoint, because the love of God has been poured
out in our hearts by the Holy Spirit who was given to us.

In His new commandment, Jesus instructed us to love others the way He loved (in the power of the Spirit), then He sent His Spirit to pour out His love in our hearts. Now we love others with God's love.

In addition to the abundance of blessings given to all of us through our inheritance, the Holy Spirit gives different gifts to each of us for use in ministry. These gifts are explained in 1 Corinthians 12:4-11.

All of us are called to share the good news of Jesus. All of us are commissioned to be ambassadors of the kingdom of heaven. All of us have been given a ministry of reconciliation. All of us are instructed to love others. And each of us will fulfill our calling and ministry differently based upon the unique gifts given to us by the Holy Spirit. We need to be careful not to judge others who do things a little differently. It may be that they are operating in different spiritual gifts than we are. Remember, Jesus overturned the tables of the moneychangers and chased them out of the Temple with a whip. And this was an acceptable function within His ministry.

Jesus promised that He would not leave us as orphans. He promised to send us the Holy Spirit to abide with us forever. He said He would never leave us or forsake us. His Spirit lives in us and goes with us everywhere we go. He is present in every activity that we participate in. We should be aware of all our actions and attitudes as well as our communication. The surrounding verses shed some light on how we should act.

Ephesians 4:29, 31-32 | NIV
Do not let any unwholesome talk come out of your mouths, but only what is helpful for building others up according to their needs, that it may benefit those who listen. Get rid of all bitterness, rage and anger, brawling and slander, along with every form of malice. Be kind and compassionate to one another, forgiving each other, just as in Christ God forgave you.

When we walk in the Spirit, we walk in light, we walk in love, and we walk in truth. God has made His home with us and has promised to never leave us nor forsake us. He has come to do life with us. If we can trust him with our eternity, surely, we can trust Him with our today.

CHAPTER 11 REVIEW QUESTIONS

1. What is the key to walking in the spirit?

2. Why did Jesus say it was to our advantage that He go away?

3. As Christians, does God's Spirit really live in us?

4. In the New Covenant, what is the temple and the dwelling place of God's presence?

5. What is *the Mystery* found in Colossians 1:27? In light of this mystery, how should we live our day to day lives?

6. What is the meaning of the Greek word *Paraklētos?* How does our relationship with *Paraklētos* help us to know the heart of God?

7. What does God's Spirit do for us when He comes?

CHAPTER 12

Blessings vs. Rewards

Under the Old Covenant, blessings were a result of Israel's good works. Obedience to the terms of that covenant was a prerequisite to receiving the blessings from God.

> *Deuteronomy 28:1-2 | NIV*
> *If you fully obey the Lord your God and carefully follow all His commands I give you today, the Lord your God will set you high above all the nations on earth. All these blessings will come on you and accompany you if you obey the Lord your God.*

Notice the two qualifiers in this passage: *if you fully obey the Lord* in verse 1 and *if you obey the Lord* in verse 2. The blessings of the Old Covenant were conditional upon Israel's response to God's instructions.

As we have already discussed, the New Covenant is not a conditional covenant. It is a completely different type of covenant called a Testament, which is a will. In God's new and better covenant, we receive God's blessings as a part of our spiritual inheritance when we enter into this relational covenant with God through the blood of Jesus. All of these blessings are a gift from God and are received by grace through faith at the point of regeneration.

As you study God's dealings with Israel, you will discover that He used blessings as a motivational tool to promote obedience and good works. This old system of good works leading to God's blessings has caused many in the church today to believe that God deals the same way with us. Many believe that if they are good enough or do a good job following the rules, then God will bless them.

Some people do not like God's plan of salvation, by grace through faith. They would rather believe that it is their righteousness that gets the into heaven, and that their good works are responsible for their eternal redemption. Religious people get angry when you tell them that their righteousness and good works have nothing to do with salvation.

He paid a debt He did not owe; I owed a debt I could not pay.

It is Jesus who is solely responsible for our salvation. He is the one who lived a perfect life. He is the one who died a perfect death. He is the one who purchased our salvation on the Cross. God has offered us eternal salvation and it has been stamped, **Paid in Full!** It is a free gift and God will not accept our good works as a form of payment. That would nullify His grace.

Why then should a Christian want to forsake the old life of sin and live a life of holiness unto God if our actions don't determine our salvation? Paul posed this question to the Christians in Rome.

Romans 6:1 | ESV
What shall we say then? Are we to continue in sin that grace may abound?

Romans 6:2 | ESV
By no means! How can we who died to sin still live in it?

Another version says, **God Forbid!** Paul says that an attitude of "it's okay to live in sin because we are under grace" is forbidden.

The New Covenant is a relational covenant similar to a marriage covenant. When we say **I do** to Jesus, it is just the beginning of an eternal relationship. We cannot enter into this covenant relationship with the attitude that says; "I'm saved and going to heaven, but I'm not concerned about holiness, righteousness, or faithfulness." That is a forbidden attitude for any believer.

The Christian life is a covenant relationship with God. If we honor that covenant, we will live a life of holiness towards God. This is not just something we do on Sundays. This is a full time committed relationship with our heavenly Father.

Many Christians today believe that there are no rules in the New Covenant, since we are not under Law, but under grace. The reality is, there are more rules, commandments, and instructions in the New Testament than in the old. The biggest difference is that our righteousness is not dependent upon our ability to perfectly follow those rules.

What then is the purpose of a believer's good works in this New Covenant?

> *Revelation 22:12 | NKJV*
> *"And behold, I am coming quickly, and My reward is with Me, to give to everyone according to his work."*

Rewards!

The first coming of Jesus was to bring God's gift of salvation. Jesus spoke these words about the reason He was initially sent to earth.

> *John 3:17 | NKJV*
> *"For God did not send His Son into the world to condemn the world, but that the world through Him might be saved"*

The second coming of Jesus will be to bring rewards to all who faithfully follow the instructions of the New Covenant. Jesus said of His second coming,

> *Matthew 16:27 | NIV*
> *"For the Son of Man is going to come in his Father's glory with his angels, and then he will reward each person according to what they have done."*

The subject of eternal rewards is covered extensively in the words of Jesus during His sermon on the mount. One of the most significant yet overlooked scriptures in His message is where He teaches that obedience to His commandments holds eternal weight in His kingdom.

> *Matthew 5:19 | NKJV*
> *"Whoever therefore breaks one of the least of these commandments, and teaches men so, shall be called least in the kingdom of heaven; but whoever does and teaches them, he shall be called great in the kingdom of heaven."*

Under the old system, obedience resulted in blessings while failure to obey the commandments resulted in curses and death. Under God's new system, our actions do not produce blessings or curses, rather eternal rewards and those rewards will directly affect our status in eternity. Jesus refers to this eternal status as, *least in the kingdom* or *great in the kingdom.*

How would you like to spend your eternity?

Rewards are intended to be a motivation to the believer to be diligent in their Christian walk. The New Covenant is full of instructions to be faithful, obedient, forgiving, loving, and a producer of good works. Our response to the commandments of Jesus will determine our heavenly social status for eternity. Our faithful service and good works will be rewarded at the second coming of Christ, and our level of reward will correlate to our authority and responsibilities in eternity. Jesus taught this concept to his followers through parables. One good example is found in *Matthew 25:14-30.*

Jesus spoke extensively about the New Covenant system of rewards in the Sermon on the Mount. He taught about rewards for right living, rewards for helping those in need, rewards for giving, rewards for prayer, and rewards for fasting. He taught that if we do these things for public recognition, then the praise of people will be our only reward, but if we do these things with the right motives to please our Father in heaven, then we will receive eternal rewards.

These are very simple yet practical instructions on how we should conduct ourselves as believers. Jesus says that when we live our Christian lives with the proper motives, we are storing up for ourselves treasures in heaven. Our good deeds become an investment in our future, being converted into spiritual equity and stored up in Heaven.

> Matthew 6:20-21| ESV
> "Lay up for yourselves treasures in heaven, where neither moth nor rust destroys and where thieves do not break in and steal. For where your treasure is, there your heart will be also."

As we live out our new identity walking in the power of the Holy Spirit, we will be storing up for ourselves eternal rewards or treasures in heaven. This may be a strange concept to some, but this is God's idea. He desires to reward the faithful workers in His kingdom.

> 1 Corinthians 3:8 | NIV
> The one who plants and the one who waters have one purpose, and they will each be rewarded according to their own labor.

This verse is referring to believers sharing the good news of Jesus with others. Anytime we play a part in the spreading of the gospel or encouraging others in their faith, we will be rewarded for our efforts.

God also offers us rewards for loving difficult people.

> *Matthew 5:46-48 | NLT*
> *"If you love only those who love you, what reward is there for that? Even corrupt tax collectors do that much. If you are kind only to your friends, how are you different from anyone else? Even pagans do that. But you are to be perfect, even as your Father in heaven is perfect."*

When we love difficult people, we experience a little bit of what it is like to be like Jesus.

And sometimes those difficult people will turn on us. The example of Jesus teaches us that one in twelve has the potential of being a Judas. We are to love them anyway.

> *Matthew 5:11-12 | NIV*
> *"Blessed are you when people insult you, persecute you and falsely say all kinds of evil against you because of me. Rejoice and be glad, because great is your reward in heaven."*

God has rewards for that, too! We receive great rewards when others speak evil of us for being a Christian.

> *Ephesians 6:7-8 | NLT*
> *Work with enthusiasm, as though you were working for the Lord rather than for people. Remember that the Lord will reward each one of us for the good we do.*

Our works will be tested! But if we have the proper motives, our works will be refined in that fire.

1 Corinthians 3:12-15 | NKJV
Now if anyone builds on this foundation with gold, silver, precious stones, wood, hay, straw, each one's work will become clear; for the Day will declare it, because it will be revealed by fire; and the fire will test each one's work, of what sort it is. If anyone's work which he has built on it endures, he will receive a reward. If anyone's work is burned, he will suffer loss; but he himself will be saved, yet so as through fire.

Let us walk in our spiritual inheritance, follow the leading of God's Holy Spirit, and be zealous for good works! In doing so we will be sure to be accepted into eternity by our heavenly Father with these words, **"Well done, good and faithful servant!"**

The final chapter in the Bible contains this promise from Jesus. Be assured, He is coming back soon!

Revelation 22:12 | NKJV
"And behold, I am coming quickly, and My reward is with Me, to give to everyone according to his work."

CHAPTER 12 REVIEW QUESTIONS

1. Under the terms of the Old Covenant, blessings were the result of what?

2. In the New Covenant, what is the difference between blessings and rewards?

3. What did Jesus say He came to bring us at His first coming?

4. What does Jesus say He will bring with Him at His second coming? Why did Jesus instruct us to *lay up treasures in heaven*?

5. What reward do we receive when we serve only to be seen by others?

6. According to *Ephesians 6:7-8,* why should we be enthusiastic about serving God?

7. Jesus is coming back soon, and He is bringing with Him rewards to recompense each of us according to our works. What manner of lives ought we to live in these last days?

CONCLUSION

I love being a Christian. Think about it: without Jesus, we are lost in our sins, spiritually dead, and destined for eternal condemnation. God sends His only Son to earth to pay the price for our sins that whoever believes in Him will not perish but have everlasting life. By simply believing in the gospel of Jesus Christ, we can enter into a covenant relationship with God. He forgives us of our sin, gives us new spiritual life, gives us a new heart, and blesses us with a spiritual inheritance. In this spiritual inheritance, we are given a new identity, blessed with every spiritual blessing and equipped with everything we need to live the Christian life. Plus, God sends us the Holy Spirit to be our Teacher, Advocate, Helper, Comforter and personal tour guide in this thing called life!

His divine power has given us everything we need for life and godliness. He has given us His life, His love, His heart, His power, and His anointing to accomplish His will for our lives. He fills us with hope, peace, and joy as he leads us in paths of righteousness. If we faithfully serve Him with all He has given to us, we shall be rewarded for all eternity! So, let's serve the Lord with all our heart, soul, mind, and strength as we share His goodness and mercy. He is worthy of all honor, glory and praise.

> *Jude 1:24-25 | NLT*
> *Now all glory to God, who is able to keep you from falling away and will bring you with great joy into His glorious presence without a single fault. All glory to Him who alone is God, our Savior through Jesus Christ our Lord. All glory, majesty, power, and authority are His before all time, and in the present, and beyond all time! Amen.*

Blessings to you all!

Printed in the United States
By Bookmasters